684040632191

GCSE
Success

Chemistry

Revision Guide

D0314563

Contents

Atoms and the periodic table

Atoms and elements
- All substances are made of **atoms**.
- An atom is the smallest part of an **element** that can exist.
- There are approximately 100 different elements, all of which are shown in the **periodic table**.

On the right is part of the periodic table, showing the names and symbols of the first 20 elements.

Atoms of each element are represented by a chemical symbol in the periodic table.

Some elements have more than one letter in their symbol. The first letter is always a capital and the other letter is lower case.

1 hydrogen **H**																	2 helium **He**
3 lithium **Li**	4 beryllium **Be**	5 boron **B**	6 carbon **C**	7 nitrogen **N**	8 oxygen **O**	9 fluorine **F**	10 neon **Ne**
11 sodium **Na**	12 magnesium **Mg**	13 aluminium **Al**	14 silicon **Si**	15 phosphorus **P**	16 sulfur **S**	17 chlorine **Cl**	18 argon **Ar**
19 potassium **K**	20 calcium **Ca**						

The symbol for magnesium is **Mg**

The symbol for the element oxygen is **O**

Elements, compounds and mixtures

Elements contain only one type of atom and consist of single atoms or atoms bonded together	Compounds contain two (or more) elements that are chemically combined in fixed proportions	Mixtures contain two or more elements (or compounds) that are together but not chemically combined

Element	Compound	Mixture

Chemical equations
We can use word or symbol equations to represent chemical reactions.

Word equation: sodium + oxygen → sodium oxide

Symbol equation: $4Na + O_2 → 2Na_2O$

Write the name of each method of separating a mixture on some cards. Use a new card for each method. Write on other cards a des... each method of se... a new card for each descri... Shuffle the cards. Now try to mat... the names and descriptions.

Separating mixtures

Compounds can only be separated by chemical reactions but **mixtures** can be separated by physical processes (not involving chemical reactions) such as filtration, crystallisation, simple (and fractional) distillation and chromatography.

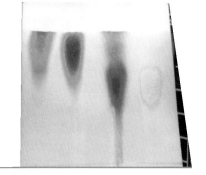

Method of separation	Diagram	Use
Filtration	Filter paper, Filter funnel, Sand and water, Sand, Beaker, Clear water (filtrate)	Used for separating insoluble solids from liquids, e.g. sand from water
Crystallisation	Evaporating dish, Mixture, Wire gauze, Tripod stand, Bunsen burner	Used to separate solids from solutions, e.g. obtaining salt from salty water
Simple distillation	Thermometer, Round-bottomed flask, Water out, Liebig condenser, Water in, Heat	Simple distillation is used to separate a liquid from a solution, e.g. water from salty water
Fractional distillation		Fractional distillation is used to separate liquids that have different boiling points, e.g. ethanol and water
Chromatography	Solvent front, Separated dyes, Filter paper, Ink spots, Pencil line, Solvent, Spot of mixture	Used to separate dyes, e.g. the different components of ink

How different mixtures can be separated

1. What name is given to a substance that contains atoms of different elements chemically joined together?
2. Which method of separation would you use to obtain water from solution of copper(II) sulfate?

Atomic structure

Scientific models of the atom

Scientists had originally thought that atoms were tiny spheres that could not be divided.

John Dalton conducted experiments in the early 19th century and concluded that…

> all matter is made of indestructible atoms
> atoms of a particular element are identical
> atoms are rearranged during chemical reactions
> compounds are formed when two or more different types of atom join together.

Upon discovery of the electron by **J. J. Thomson** in 1897, the 'plum pudding' model suggested that the atom was a ball of positive charge with negative electrons embedded throughout.

The results from **Rutherford**, **Geiger** and **Marsden's** alpha scattering experiments (1911–1913) led to the plum pudding model being replaced by the nuclear model.

In this experiment, alpha particles (which are positive) are fired at a thin piece of gold. A few of the alpha particles do not pass through the gold and are deflected. Most went straight through the thin piece of gold. This led Rutherford, Geiger and Marsden to suggest that this is because the positive charge of the atom is confined in a small volume (now called the nucleus).

Niels Bohr adapted the nuclear model in 1913, by suggesting that electrons orbit the nucleus at specific distances. Bohr's theoretical calculations were backed up by experimental results.

Later experiments led to the idea that the positive charge of the nucleus was subdivided into smaller particles (now called protons), with each particle having the same amount of positive charge.

The work of **James Chadwick** suggested in 1932 that the nucleus also contained neutral particles that we now call neutrons.

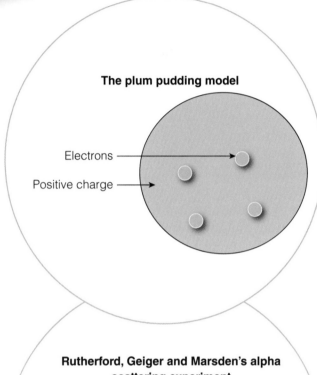

The plum pudding model

Electrons

Positive charge

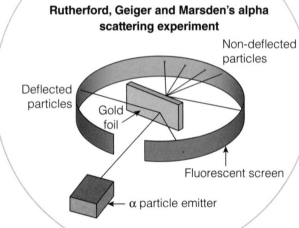

Rutherford, Geiger and Marsden's alpha scattering experiment

Non-deflected particles

Deflected particles

Gold foil

Fluorescent screen

α particle emitter

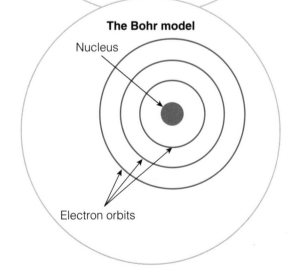

The Bohr model

Nucleus

Electron orbits

Properties of atoms

Particle	Relative charge	Relative mass
Proton	+1	1
Neutron	0	1
Electron	−1	negligible

➤ Atoms are neutral. This is because the number of protons is equal to the number of electrons.

➤ Atoms of different elements have different numbers of protons. This number is called the atomic number.

➤ Atoms are very small, having a radius of approximately 0.1 nm (1×10^{-10} m).

➤ The radius of the nucleus is approximately $\frac{1}{10\,000}$ of the size of the atom.

> The **mass number** tells you the total number of protons and neutrons in an atom

$$^{23}_{11}Na$$

> The **atomic number** tells you the number of protons in an atom

mass number – atomic number = number of neutrons

Some atoms can have different numbers of neutrons. These atoms are called **isotopes**. The existence of isotopes results in the relative atomic mass of some elements, e.g. chlorine, not being whole numbers.

HT Chlorine exists as two isotopes. Chlorine-35 makes up 75% of all chlorine atoms. Chlorine-37 makes up the other 25%. We say that the abundance of chlorine-35 is 75%.

The relative atomic mass of chlorine can be calculated as follows:

$$\frac{(\text{mass of isotope 1} \times \text{abundance}) + (\text{mass of isotope 2} \times \text{abundance})}{100}$$

$$= \frac{(35 \times 75) + (37 \times 25)}{100} = 35.5$$

Keywords

Mass number ➤ The total number of protons and neutrons in an atom

Atomic number ➤ The number of protons in the nucleus of an atom

Isotopes ➤ Atoms of the same element that have the same number of protons but different numbers of neutrons

Make models of atoms using different coloured paper to represent the protons, neutrons and electrons.

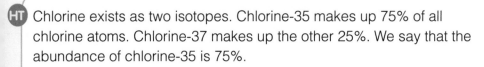

1. What is the difference between the plum pudding model of the atom and the nuclear model of the atom?
2. Why did Rutherford, Geiger and Marsden's alpha scattering experiment lead them to suggest that the positive charge in an atom was contained within a small volume?
3. How many protons, neutrons and electrons are present in the following atom?

$$^{13}_{6}C$$

4. What name is given to atoms of the same element which have the same number of protons but different numbers of neutrons?

Electronic structure & the periodic table

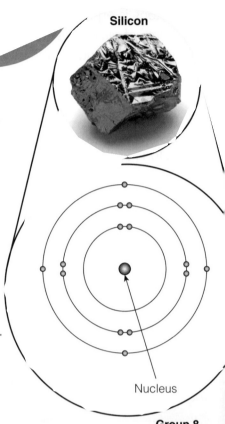

Silicon

Electronic structures

Electrons in an atom occupy the lowest available **energy level** (**shell**). The first energy level (closest to the nucleus) can hold up to two electrons. The second and third energy levels can hold up to eight electrons.

For example, silicon has the atomic number 14. This means that there are 14 protons in the nucleus of a silicon atom and therefore there must be 14 electrons (so that the atom is neutral).

The electronic structure of silicon can be written as 2, 8, 4 or shown in a diagram like the one on the right.

Silicon is in group 4 of the periodic table. This is because it has four electrons in its outer shell. The chemical properties (reactions) of an element are related to the number of electrons in the outer shell of the atom.

The electronic structure of the first 20 elements are shown here.

Nucleus

Group 1	Group 2			Group 3	Group 4	Group 5	Group 6	Group 7	Group 8
		Hydrogen, H Atomic No. = 1 No. of electrons = 1 — 1							**Helium, He** Atomic No. = 2 No. of electrons = 2 — 2
Lithium, Li Atomic No. = 3 No. of electrons = 3 — 2, 1	**Beryllium, Be** Atomic No. = 4 No. of electrons = 4 — 2, 2			**Boron, B** Atomic No. = 5 No. of electrons = 5 — 2, 3	**Carbon, C** Atomic No. = 6 No. of electrons = 6 — 2, 4	**Nitrogen, N** Atomic No. = 7 No. of electrons = 7 — 2, 5	**Oxygen, O** Atomic No. = 8 No. of electrons = 8 — 2, 6	**Fluorine, F** Atomic No. = 9 No. of electrons = 9 — 2, 7	**Neon, Ne** Atomic No. = 10 No. of electrons = 10 — 2, 8
Sodium, Na Atomic No. = 11 No. of electrons = 11 — 2, 8, 1	**Magnesium, Mg** Atomic No. = 12 No. of electrons = 12 — 2, 8, 2			**Aluminium, Al** Atomic No. = 13 No. of electrons = 13 — 2, 8, 3	**Silicon, Si** Atomic No. = 14 No. of electrons = 14 — 2, 8, 4	**Phosphorus, P** Atomic No. = 15 No. of electrons = 15 — 2, 8, 5	**Sulfur, S** Atomic No. = 16 No. of electrons = 16 — 2, 8, 6	**Chlorine, Cl** Atomic No. = 17 No. of electrons = 17 — 2, 8, 7	**Argon, Ar** Atomic No. = 18 No. of electrons = 18 — 2, 8, 8
Potassium, K Atomic No. = 19 No. of electrons = 19 — 2, 8, 8, 1	**Calcium, Ca** Atomic No. = 20 No. of electrons = 20 — 2, 8, 8, 2	**THE TRANSITION METALS**							

This table is arranged in order of atomic (proton) numbers, placing the elements in groups. Elements in the same group have the same number of electrons in their highest occupied energy level (outer shell).

The electron configuration of oxygen is 2, 6 because there are…
- 2 electrons in the first shell
- 6 electrons in the second shell.

The periodic table

The elements in the periodic table are arranged in order of increasing atomic (proton) number.
The table is called a **periodic table** because similar properties occur at regular intervals.

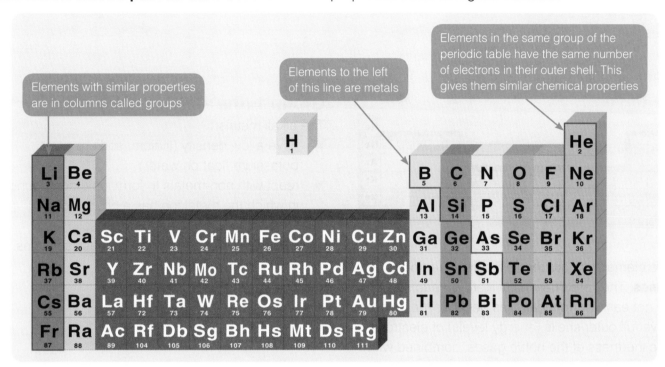

Elements with similar properties are in columns called groups

Elements to the left of this line are metals

Elements in the same group of the periodic table have the same number of electrons in their outer shell. This gives them similar chemical properties

Development of the periodic table

Before the discovery of protons, neutrons and electrons, early attempts to classify the elements involved placing them in order of their atomic weights. These early attempts resulted in incomplete tables and the placing of some elements in appropriate groups based on their chemical properties.

Dmitri Mendeleev overcame some of these problems by leaving gaps for elements that he predicted were yet to be discovered. He also changed the order for some elements based on atomic weights. Knowledge of isotopes made it possible to explain why the order based on atomic weights was not always correct.

Metals and non-metals

➤ Metals are elements that react to form positive ions.
➤ Elements that do not form positive ions are non-metals.

Typical properties of metals and non-metals	
Metals	Non-metals
Have high melting / boiling points	Have low melting / boiling points
Conduct heat and electricity	Thermal and electrical insulators
React with oxygen to form alkalis	React with oxygen to form acids
Shiny	Dull
Malleable and ductile	Brittle

a model of an
n of one of the first
elements. Make
sure that you have
umber of

as the atomic number 11. What is   structure of sodium?
d Mendeleev leave gaps in his periodic table?
ent X has a high melting point, is malleable and conducts electricity. Is X a metal or a
n-metal?

Groups 0, 1 and 7

Group 0

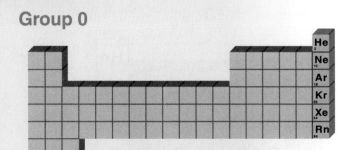

The elements in group 0 are called the **noble gases**. They are chemically inert (unreactive) and do not easily form molecules because their atoms have full outer shells (energy levels) of electrons. The inertness of the noble gases, combined with their low density and non-flammability, mean that they can be used in airships, balloons, light bulbs, lasers and advertising signs.

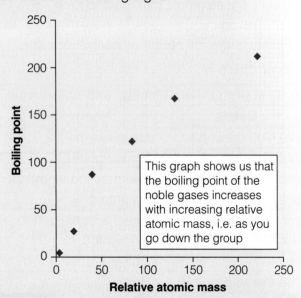

This graph shows us that the boiling point of the noble gases increases with increasing relative atomic mass, i.e. as you go down the group

Group 1 (the alkali metals)

The alkali metals…

➤ have a low density (lithium, sodium and potassium float on water)
➤ react with non-metals to form ionic compounds in which the metal ion has a charge of +1
➤ form compounds that are white solids and dissolve in water to form colourless solutions.

The alkali metals react with water forming metal hydroxides which dissolve in water to form alkaline solutions and hydrogen gas. For example, for the reaction between sodium and water:

$$2Na_{(s)} + 2H_2O_{(l)} \rightarrow 2NaOH_{(aq)} + H_{2(g)}$$

The alkali metals become more reactive as you go down the group because the outer shell gets further away from the positive attraction of the nucleus. This makes it easier for an atom to lose an electron from its outer shell.

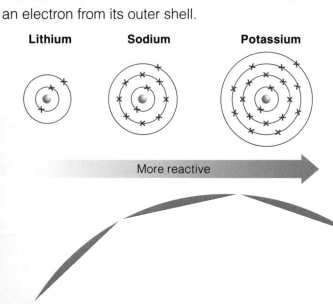

Lithium   **Sodium**   **Potassium**

More reactive

Write each property of the alkali metals and the halogens on separate cards. Shuffle the cards. Now try to place them into the correct two piles: **alkali metals** and **halogens**.

Group 7 (the halogens)

The **halogens**…

➤ are non-metals
➤ consist of diatomic molecules (molecules made up of two atoms)
➤ react with metals to form ionic compounds where the halide ion has a charge of –1
➤ form molecular compounds with other non-metals
➤ form hydrogen halides (e.g. HCl), which dissolve in water, forming acidic solutions.

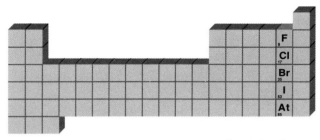

Crystals of natural fluorite

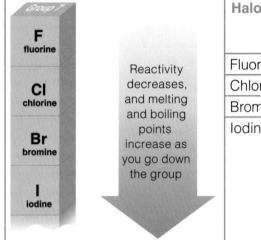

Halogen	State of matter at room temperature	Colour
Fluorine	Gas	Yellow
Chlorine	Gas	Green
Bromine	Liquid	Red / orange
Iodine	Solid	Grey / black

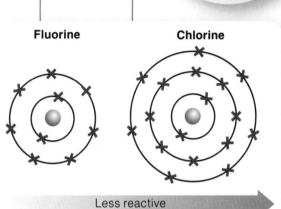

Halogens become less reactive as you go down the group because the outer electron shell gets further away from the attraction of the nucleus, and so an electron is gained less easily.

Displacement reactions of halogens

A more reactive halogen will **displace** a less reactive halogen from an aqueous solution of its metal halide.

For example:

chlorine + potassium bromide → potassium chloride + bromine
Cl_2 + 2KBr → 2KCl + Br_2

The products of reactions between halogens and aqueous solutions of halide ion salts are as follows.

		Halide salts	
	Potassium chloride, KCl	Potassium bromide, KBr	Potassium iodide, KI
Halogens Chlorine, Cl_2	No reaction	Potassium chloride + bromine	Potassium chloride + iodine
Bromine, Br_2	No reaction	No reaction	Potassium bromide + iodine
Iodine, I_2	No reaction	No reaction	No reaction

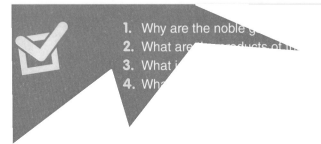

1. Why are the noble g
2. What are the products of
3. What i
4. Wha

Transition metals

5

Comparison with group 1 elements

Typical transition metals are chromium, manganese, iron, cobalt, nickel and copper.

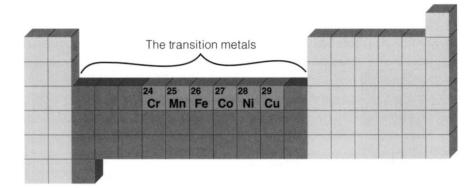

The transition metals

24	25	26	27	28	29
Cr	Mn	Fe	Co	Ni	Cu

Chromium car exhaust pipes

Manganese

Copper

Nickel coins

Compared with group 1 metals, the transition metals....
- ➤ have higher melting points (except for mercury)
- ➤ are more dense
- ➤ are less reactive with water and oxygen

Properties of transition metals

Many transition elements have ions with different charges. For example, $FeCl_2$ is a compound that contains Fe^{2+} ions and $FeCl_3$ is a compound that contains Fe^{3+} ions.

Compounds of transition metals are also often coloured. For example, potassium manganate(VII), $KMnO_4$, is purple and copper(II) sulfate, $CuSO_4$, is blue.

Keywords

Catalyst ➤ A substance that changes the rate of a chemical reaction without being used up or chemically changed at the end of the reaction

Haber process ➤ A process used to make ammonia, NH_3

The purple colour of potassium manganate(VII) solution

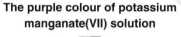

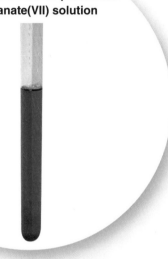

The colours of some other transition metal ions

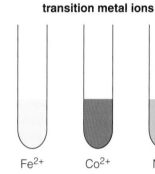

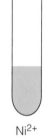

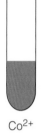

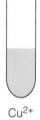

Cr3+
Fe2+
Co2+
Ni2+
Cu2+

Transition metals are also frequently used as **catalysts**, such as iron in the **Haber process** (see Module 40) and nickel used in the manufacture of margarine.

Margarine

Iron ore

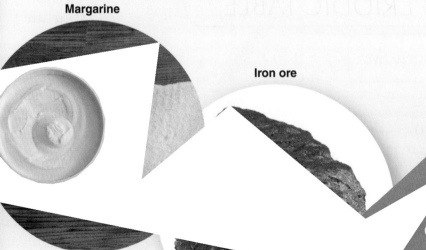

Colour paper in different colours corresponding to the colours of the different transition metal ions shown on this page. On the reverse of the paper, write the ion that provides this colour.

...s of transition metals when compared with group 1 metals.
...of a transition metal compound.
...catalyst in the Haber process?

Mind map

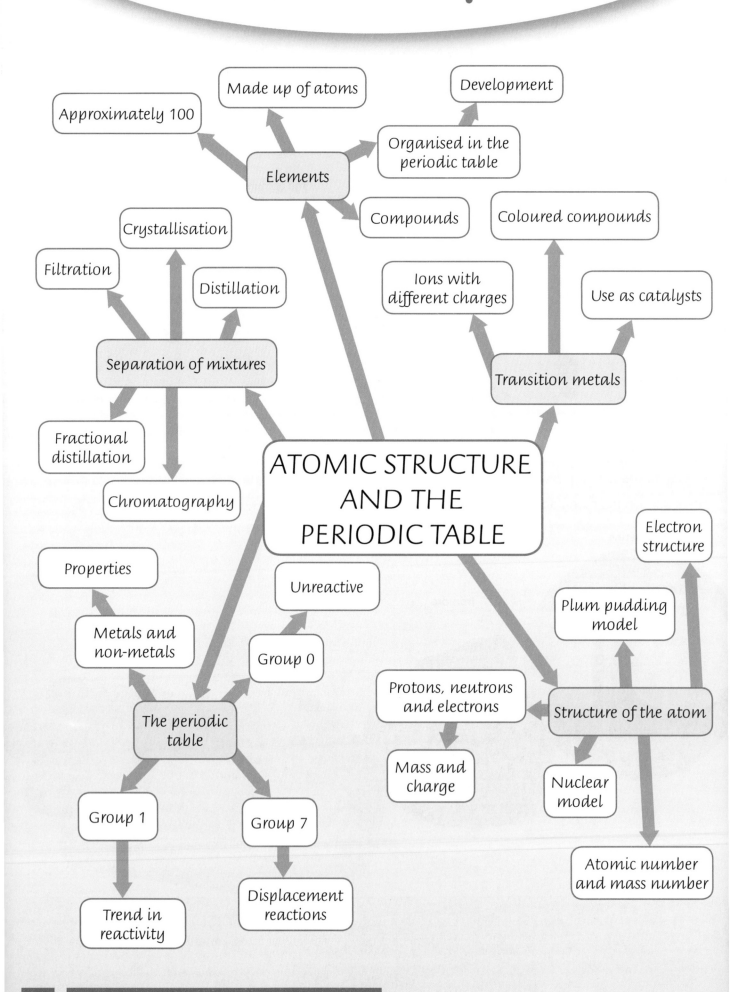

Approximately 100

Made up of atoms

Development

Organised in the periodic table

Elements

Compounds

Coloured compounds

Crystallisation

Filtration

Distillation

Ions with different charges

Use as catalysts

Separation of mixtures

Transition metals

Fractional distillation

ATOMIC STRUCTURE AND THE PERIODIC TABLE

Chromatography

Properties

Unreactive

Electron structure

Plum pudding model

Metals and non-metals

Group 0

Protons, neutrons and electrons

Structure of the atom

The periodic table

Mass and charge

Nuclear model

Group 1

Group 7

Atomic number and mass number

Trend in reactivity

Displacement reactions

Practice questions

1. This question is about the non-metal chlorine.

   An atom of chlorine can be represented as:

   $$^{35}_{17}Cl$$

   a) Give the number of protons, neutrons and electrons in an atom of chlorine. **(3 marks)**

   b) What is the electronic structure of chlorine? **(1 mark)**

   c) Chlorine exists as two isotopes.
   The other isotope of chlorine is represented as:

   $$^{37}_{17}Cl$$

   Give one similarity and one difference between the two isotopes of chlorine. **(2 marks)**

   d) Give one property of chlorine that is characteristic of it being a non-metal. **(1 mark)**

   e) Write a balanced symbol equation for the reaction between chlorine and sodium iodide solution. **(2 marks)**

   f) Explain why chlorine does not react with sodium fluoride solution. **(2 marks)**

2. Sand does not dissolve in water but salt does.

   a) How can sand be separated from water? **(1 mark)**

   b) Draw and label a diagram to show how water can be collected from a salt water solution. **(3 marks)**

   c) Why is crystallisation not a suitable method for obtaining water from a salt water solution? **(1 mark)**

3. The element boron exists as two naturally occurring isotopes. The mass and abundance (amount) of each isotope of boron is shown below.

Mass number of isotope	% abundance
10	20
11	80

   Use the above information to calculate the relative atomic mass of boron.
   Give your answer to three significant figures. **(3 marks)**

Chemical bonding

There are three types of chemical bond:

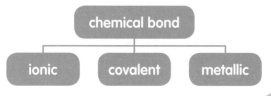

Ionic bonding

Ionic bonds occur between metals and non-metals. An ionic bond is the electrostatic force of attraction between two oppositely charged **ions** (called **cations** and **anions**).

Ionic bonds are formed when metal atoms transfer electrons to non-metal atoms. This is done so that each atom forms an ion with a full outer shell of electrons.

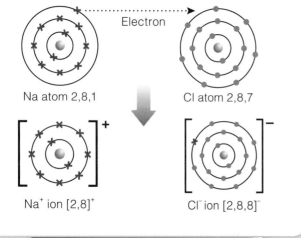

Example 1: The formation of an ionic bond between sodium and chlorine

Na atom 2,8,1 — Electron → Cl atom 2,8,7

Na⁺ ion [2,8]⁺ — Cl⁻ ion [2,8,8]⁻

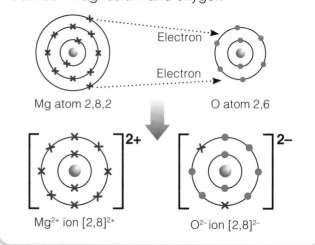

Example 2: The formation of the ionic bond between magnesium and oxygen

Mg atom 2,8,2 — Electron, Electron → O atom 2,6

Mg²⁺ ion [2,8]²⁺ — O²⁻ ion [2,8]²⁻

Covalent bonding

Covalent bonds occur between two non-metal atoms. Atoms share a pair of electrons so that each atom ends up with a full outer shell of electrons, such as:

➤ the formation of a covalent bond between two hydrogen atoms

Hydrogen atoms   **A hydrogen molecule**

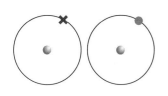 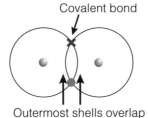

Covalent bond

Outermost shells overlap

➤ the covalent bonding in methane, CH_4.

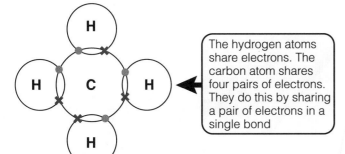

The hydrogen atoms share electrons. The carbon atom shares four pairs of electrons. They do this by sharing a pair of electrons in a single bond

Double covalent bonds occur when two pairs of electrons are shared between atoms, for example in carbon dioxide.

Carbon dioxide

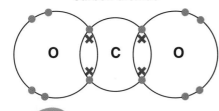

Keywords

Ion ➤ An atom or group of atoms that has gained or lost one or more electrons in order to gain a full outer shell
Cation ➤ A positive ion
Anion ➤ A negative ion
Delocalised electrons ➤ Free-moving electrons

Metallic bonding

Metals consist of giant structures. Each atom loses its outer shell electrons and these electrons become **delocalised**, i.e. they are free to move through the structure. The metal cations are arranged in a regular pattern called a lattice (see below).

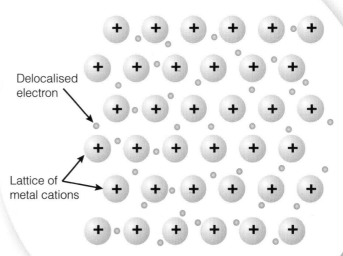

Delocalised electron

Lattice of metal cations

Use the models of atoms you have previously made to try to work out what happens when different atoms bond together. Make sure that each atom ends up with a full outer shell. Remember that you might need more than one of each type of atom.

1. What type of bonding occurs between a metal and non-metal atom?
2. How many electrons are present in every covalent bond?
3. Describe the structure of a metal.

Ionic and covalent structures

Structure of ionic compounds

Compounds containing ionic bonds form giant structures. These are held together by strong electrostatic forces of attraction between the oppositely charged ions. These forces act in all directions throughout the lattice.

The diagram below represents a typical giant ionic structure, sodium chloride.

Sodium chloride

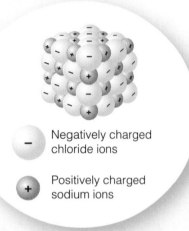

– Negatively charged chloride ions

+ Positively charged sodium ions

The ratio of each ion present in the structure allows the **empirical formula** of the compound to be worked out. In the diagram above, there are equal numbers of sodium ions and chloride ions. This means that the empirical formula is NaCl.

Structure of covalent compounds

Covalently bonded substances may consist of....
➤ small molecules / simple molecular structures (e.g. Cl_2, H_2O and CH_4)
➤ large molecules (e.g. **polymers** – see Module 28)
➤ giant covalent structures (e.g. diamond, graphite and silicon dioxide).

Small molecular structures

The bonding between hydrogen and carbon in methane can be represented in several ways, as shown here.

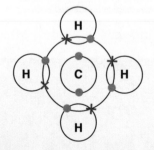

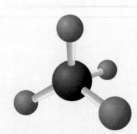

Large molecules

Polymers can be represented in the form:

$$\left[\begin{array}{cc} V & W \\ | & | \\ -C-C- \\ | & | \\ Y & X \end{array} \right]_n$$

V, W, X and Y represent the atoms bonded to the carbon atoms

For example, poly(ethene) can be represented as:

$$\left[\begin{array}{cc} H & H \\ | & | \\ -C-C- \\ | & | \\ H & H \end{array} \right]_n$$

Giant covalent structures

This is the giant covalent structure of silicon dioxide.

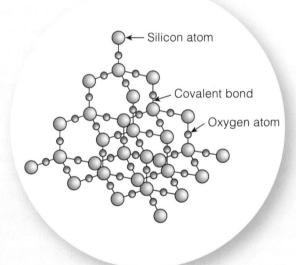

Silicon atom

Covalent bond

Oxygen atom

Keywords

Empirical formula ➤ The simplest whole number ratio of each kind of atom present in a compound

Polymer ➤ A large, long-chained molecule

Make a model that represents sodium chloride or silicon dioxide. Count the number of each particle and then work out the simplest whole number ratio of each particle present. This is the empirical formula.

Diamond

The formula of silicon dioxide is SiO_2 – this can be deduced by looking at the ratio of Si to O atoms in the diagram above.

Models, such as dot-and-cross diagrams, ball-and-stick diagrams and two- / three-dimensional diagrams to represent structures, are limited in value, as they do not accurately represent the structures of materials. For example, a chemical bond is not a solid object as depicted in some models, it is actually an attraction between particles. The relative size of different atoms is often not shown when drawing diagrams.

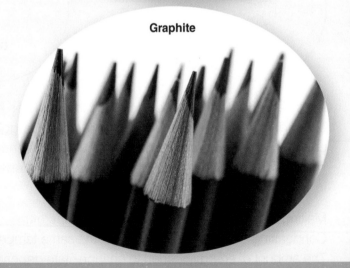

Graphite

1. What forces hold ionic structures together?
2. What are the three types of covalent substance?
3. Draw a diagram to show the structure of sodium chloride.

States of matter: properties of compounds

States of matter

The three main states of matter are **solids**, **liquids** and **gases**. Individual atoms do not have the same properties as these bulk substances. The diagram below shows how they can be interconverted and also how the particles in the different states of matter are arranged.

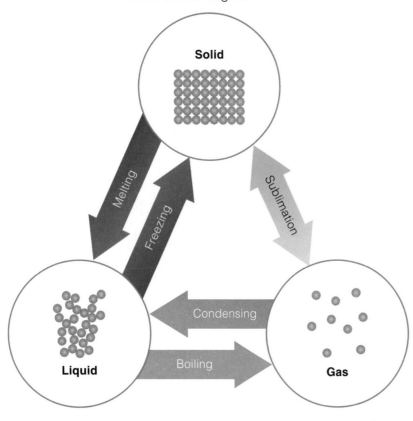

These are physical changes because the particles are either gaining or losing energy and are not undergoing a chemical reaction. Particles in a gas have more energy than in a liquid; particles in a liquid would have more energy than in a solid.

Melting and freezing occur at the same temperature. Condensing and boiling also occur at the same temperature. The amount of energy needed to change state depends on the strength of the forces between the particles of the substance.

The stronger the forces between the particles, the higher the melting and boiling points of the substance.

Properties of ionic compounds	
Property	Explanation
High melting and boiling points	There are lots of strong bonds throughout an ionic lattice which require lots of energy to break.
Electrical conductivity	Ionic compounds conduct electricity when molten or dissolved in water because the ions are free to move and carry the charge. Ionic solids do not conduct electricity because the ions are in a fixed position and are unable to move.

HT The model on the left is limited in value because….
- it does not indicate that there are forces between the spheres
- all particles are represented as spheres
- the spheres are solid.

Keyword

Intermolecular forces ➤ The weak forces of attraction that occur between molecules

Properties of small molecules

Substances made up of small molecules are usually gases or liquids at room temperature. They have relatively low melting and boiling points because there are weak (intermolecular) forces that act between the molecules. It is these weak forces and not the strong covalent bonds that are broken when the substance melts or boils.

Substances made up of small molecules do not normally conduct electricity. This is because the molecules do not have an overall electric charge or delocalised electrons.

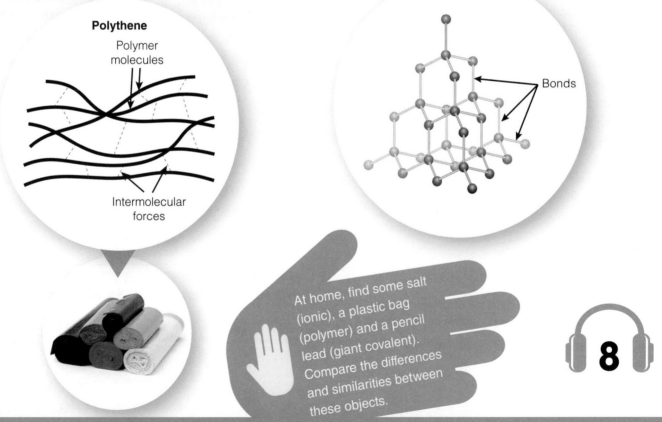

Polymers

Polymers are very large molecules made up of atoms joined together by strong covalent bonds. The intermolecular forces between polymer molecules are much stronger than in small molecules because the molecules are larger. This is why most polymers are solid at room temperature.

Giant covalent structures

Substances with a giant covalent structure are solids at room temperature. They have relatively high melting and boiling points. This is because there are lots of strong covalent bonds that need to be broken.

At home, find some salt (ionic), a plastic bag (polymer) and a pencil lead (giant covalent). Compare the differences and similarities between these objects.

🎧 **8**

1. What is the main factor that determines the melting point of a solid?
2. Why do ionic compounds have relatively high melting points?
3. What needs to be broken in order to melt a substance made up of small molecules such as water?
4. Why do polymers have higher melting points than substances made up of small molecules?
5. Why do substances with giant covalent structures have relatively high melting points?

Metals, alloys & the structure and bonding of carbon

9

Structure and properties of metals

Metals have giant structures. Metallic bonding (the attraction between the cations and the delocalised electrons) is strong meaning that most metals have high melting and boiling points.

The layers are able to slide over each other, which means that metals can be bent and shaped.

Metals are good conductors of electricity because the delocalised electrons are able to move.

The delocalised electrons also transfer energy meaning that they are good thermal conductors.

High melting point

Strong forces of attraction between cations and electrons

Malleable

Force applied

Force applied

Rows of ions slide over each other

Electrons moving between the cations

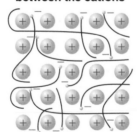

Alloys

Most metals we use are **alloys**. Many pure metals (such as gold, iron and aluminium) are too soft for many uses and so are mixed with other materials (usually metals) to make alloys.

The different sizes of atoms in alloys make it difficult for the layers to slide over each other. This is why alloys are harder than pure metals.

Typical alloy structure

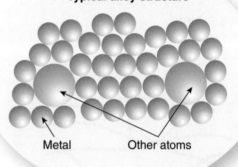

Metal   Other atoms

Structure and bonding of carbon

Carbon has four different structures.

carbon

diamond   graphite   graphene   fullerenes

Keywords

Alloy ➤ A mixture of two or more metals, or a mixture of a metal and a non-metal

Fullerene ➤ A molecule made of carbon atoms arranged as a hollow sphere

Nanotube ➤ A molecule made of carbon atoms arranged in a tubular structure

High tensile strength ➤ Does not break easily when stretched

Diamond

Diamond is a giant covalent structure (or macromolecule) where each carbon atom is bonded to four others.

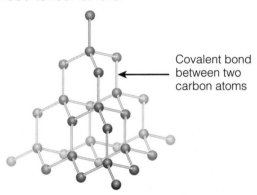

Covalent bond between two carbon atoms

In diamond, there are lots of very strong covalent bonds so diamond…

➤ is hard
➤ has a high melting point.

For these reasons, diamond is used in making cutting tools.

There are no free electrons in diamond so it does not conduct electricity.

Graphite

Graphite is also a giant covalent structure, with each carbon atom forming three covalent bonds, resulting in layers of hexagonal rings of carbon atoms. Carbon has four electrons in its outer shell and as only three are used for bonding the other one is delocalised.

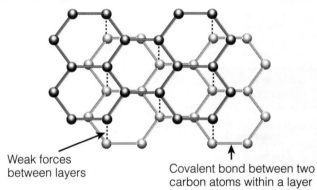

Weak forces between layers

Covalent bond between two carbon atoms within a layer

The layers in graphite are able to slide over each other because there are only weak intermolecular forces holding them together. This is why graphite is soft and slippery. These properties make graphite suitable for use as a lubricant.

Like diamond, there are lots of strong covalent bonds in graphite so it has a high melting point.

The delocalised electrons allow graphite to conduct electricity and heat.

Graphene and fullerenes

Graphene is a single layer of graphite and so it is one atom thick.

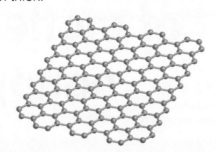

Fullerenes are molecules made up of carbon atoms and they have hollow shapes. The structure of fullerenes is based on hexagonal rings of carbon atoms but they may also contain rings with five or seven carbon atoms.

buckminsterfullerene (C_{60}) was the first fullerene to be discovered

Carbon **nanotubes** are cylindrical fullerenes.

Fullerenes have high…

➤ **tensile strength**
➤ electrical conductivity
➤ thermal conductivity.

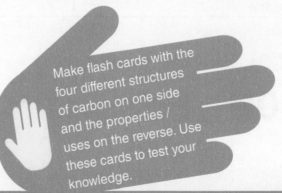

Fullerenes can be used…

➤ for drug delivery into the body
➤ as lubricants
➤ for reinforcing materials, e.g. tennis rackets.

Make flash cards with the four different structures of carbon on one side and the properties / uses on the reverse. Use these cards to test your knowledge.

1. Why do metals generally have high melting points?
2. Why are alloys harder than pure metals?
3. Why does graphite conduct electricity?
4. State two properties of fullerenes.
5. Give two uses of fullerenes.

Bulk and surface properties of matter, including nanoparticles

(WS) Sizes of particles

Nanoscience is the study of structures that are 1–100 **nanometres** (nm) in size, i.e. a few hundred atoms.

Name of particle	Diameter of particles
Coarse particles / dust (PM_{10})	Between 1×10^{-5} and 2.5×10^{-6} m
Fine particles ($PM_{2.5}$)	Between 1×10^{-7} and 2.5×10^{-6} m (100 and 250 nm)
Nanoparticles	Less than 1×10^{-7} m (100 nm)

PM = particulate matter

As the side of a cube decreases by a factor of 10, the surface area to volume ratio $\left(\dfrac{\text{surface area}}{\text{volume}}\right)$ increases by a factor of 10.

length of side	10	1
surface area	$10 \times 10 \times 6 = 600$	$1 \times 1 \times 6 = 6$
volume	$10 \times 10 \times 10 = 1000$	$1 \times 1 \times 1 = 1$
$\dfrac{\text{surface area}}{\text{volume}}$	0.6	6

Length of side decreases by a factor of 10

Surface area to volume ratio increases by a factor of 10

Properties of nanoparticles

Nanoparticles may have properties that are different from larger amounts of the same material because of their higher surface area to volume ratio. This may mean that smaller quantities are needed to be effective when compared with materials which have normal-sized particles.

Keywords

Nanoscience ➤ The study of structures that are 1–100 nm in size (i.e. a few hundred atoms)

Nanometre ➤ 1×10^{-9} (0.000 000 001) m

Nanoparticles ➤ Particles that are less than 100 nm in size

Uses of nanoparticles

In deodorants and fabrics to prevent the growth of bacteria

Controlled drug delivery

Development of new catalysts for fuel cell materials

Uses of nanoparticles

Cosmetics and sun creams

Synthetic skin

Electronics

Use of nanoparticles in sun creams	
Advantages	**Disadvantages**
Better skin coverage	Potential cell damage in the body
More effective protection from the Sun's ultraviolet rays	Potentially harmful effects on the environment

Make one small and one large cube out of paper. Now calculate the total surface area, volume of each cube and the surface area to volume ratio.

1. What size are nanoparticles?
2. What happens to the surface area to volume ratio of a cube when the side of a cube decreases by a factor of 10?
3. State two uses of nanoparticles.
4. Give one advantage and one disadvantage of using nanoparticles in sun creams.

Mind map

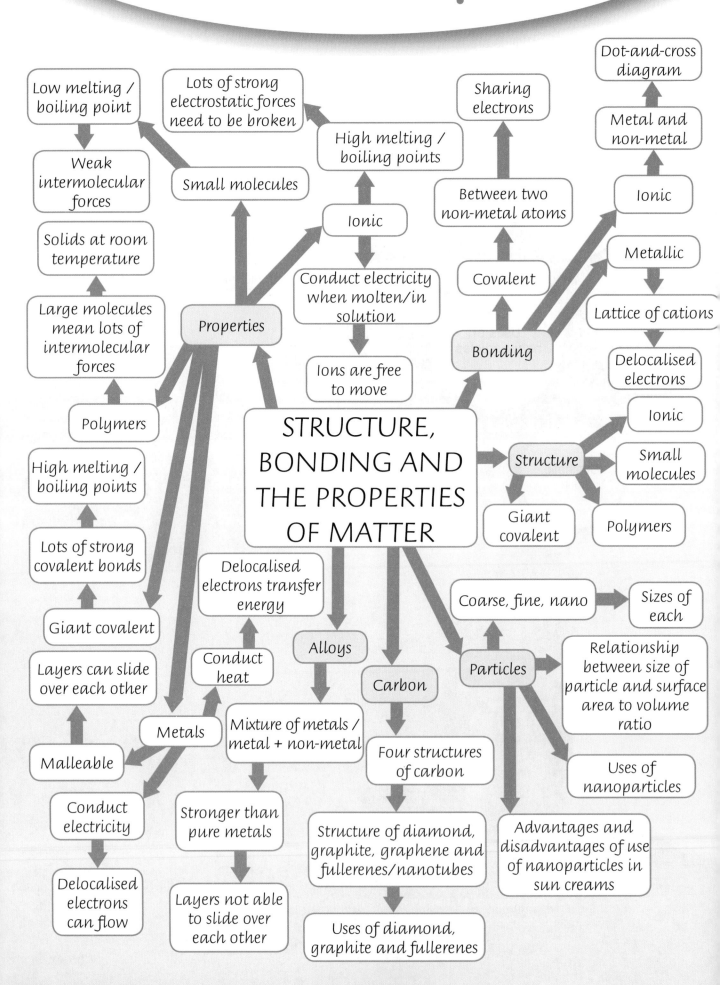

Low melting / boiling point

Lots of strong electrostatic forces need to be broken

Sharing electrons

Dot-and-cross diagram

Weak intermolecular forces

Small molecules

High melting / boiling points

Metal and non-metal

Solids at room temperature

Ionic

Between two non-metal atoms

Ionic

Large molecules mean lots of intermolecular forces

Properties

Conduct electricity when molten/in solution

Covalent

Metallic

Lattice of cations

Bonding

Polymers

Ions are free to move

Delocalised electrons

High melting / boiling points

STRUCTURE, BONDING AND THE PROPERTIES OF MATTER

Ionic

Lots of strong covalent bonds

Structure

Small molecules

Giant covalent

Giant covalent

Delocalised electrons transfer energy

Polymers

Layers can slide over each other

Conduct heat

Alloys

Carbon

Coarse, fine, nano

Sizes of each

Particles

Relationship between size of particle and surface area to volume ratio

Malleable

Metals

Mixture of metals / metal + non-metal

Conduct electricity

Stronger than pure metals

Four structures of carbon

Uses of nanoparticles

Delocalised electrons can flow

Layers not able to slide over each other

Structure of diamond, graphite, graphene and fullerenes/nanotubes

Advantages and disadvantages of use of nanoparticles in sun creams

Uses of diamond, graphite and fullerenes

Practice questions

1. This question is about the structure and bonding of sodium chloride and the properties that it has.

   a) What type of bonding is present in sodium chloride? **(1 mark)**

   b) Draw a dot-and-cross diagram to show the formation of the bond in sodium chloride. Draw the electronic structure of the atoms before the bond has formed and the ions after the bond has formed. **(3 marks)**

   c) Explain how the ions in sodium chloride are held together. **(2 marks)**

   d) Does sodium chloride have a high or a low boiling point? Explain your answer. **(2 marks)**

   e) Draw a diagram showing the positions of the ions in a crystal of sodium chloride. **(1 mark)**

2. Carbon dioxide and silicon dioxide have different structures.

   a) What type of bonding is present in both carbon dioxide and silicon dioxide? **(1 mark)**

   b) The diagram below shows the bonding in carbon dioxide.

   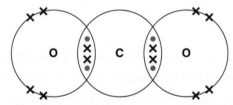

      i) How many covalent bonds are there between the carbon atom and each oxygen atom? **(1 mark)**

      ii) Does carbon dioxide have a simple molecular or giant covalent (macromolecular) structure? **(1 mark)**

   c) The structure of silicon dioxide is shown below.

   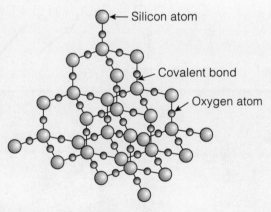

      i) Does silicon dioxide have a simple molecular or a giant covalent (macromolecular) structure? **(1 mark)**

      ii) In terms of structure, what is the difference between a simple molecular structure and a giant covalent (macromolecular) structure? **(2 marks)**

   d) Would you expect silicon dioxide to have a higher or lower boiling point than carbon dioxide? Explain your answer. **(2 marks)**

Mass and equations

Conservation of mass

The total mass of reactants in a chemical reaction is equal to the total mass of the products because atoms are not created or destroyed.

Chemical reactions are represented by balanced symbol equations.

For example:

This means there are four atoms of Na ➤ $4Na + TiCl_4 \rightarrow 4NaCl + Ti$

This means there are four atoms of chlorine in $TiCl_4$

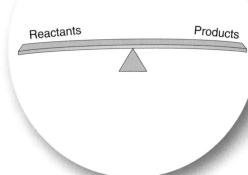

Reactants   Products

Relative formula mass

The **relative formula mass** (M_r) of a compound is the sum of the relative atomic masses (see the periodic table on page 104) of the atoms in the formula.

For example:
- The M_r of MgO is 40 $\quad$ (24 + 16)
- The M_r of H_2SO_4 is 98 $\quad$ [(2 × 1) + 32 + (4 × 16)]

In a balanced symbol equation, the sum of the relative formula masses of the reactants equals the sum of the relative formula masses of the products.

Example: $\quad\quad\quad\quad CaCO_3 + 2HCl \rightarrow CaCl_2 + H_2O + CO_2$

Sum of relative formula masses: $\quad$ 100 + (2 × 36.5) = 173 $\quad\quad$ 111 + 18 + 44 = 173

Mass changes when a reactant or product is a gas

During some chemical reactions, there can appear to be a change in mass. When copper is heated its mass actually increases because oxygen is being added to it.

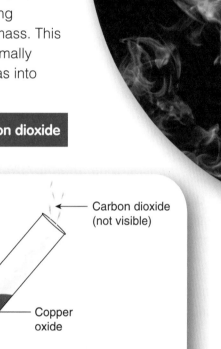

Copper

copper + oxygen → copper oxide

The mass of copper oxide formed is equal to the starting mass of copper plus the mass of the oxygen that has been added to it.

During a **thermal decomposition** reaction of a metal carbonate, the final mass of remaining metal oxide solid is less than the starting mass. This is because when the metal carbonate thermally decomposes it releases carbon dioxide gas into the atmosphere.

copper carbonate → copper oxide + carbon dioxide

Copper carbonate

Heat

Carbon dioxide (not visible)

Copper oxide

Example:

Starting mass of copper carbonate	= 8.00 g
Final mass of copper oxide	= 5.15 g
Therefore, mass of carbon dioxide released to the atmosphere	= 2.85 g (8.00 g – 5.15 g)

Make cards with the symbol of the element on one side and the relative atomic mass on the reverse.
Use these cards to work out the relative formula mass of the compounds you find in this book.

1. In a chemical reaction the total mass of reactants is 13.60 g. Will the expected mass of all the products be lower, higher or the same as 13.60 g?
2. With reference to the periodic table on page 104 work out the relative formula mass of the following compounds.
   a) NH_4NO_3
   b) $Mg(OH)_2$
3. When 5.0 g of zinc carbonate is heated will the mass of remaining metal oxide be lower, higher or the same as 5.0 g?

Moles and masses

Moles and Avogadro's constant

Amounts of chemicals are measured in **moles** (mol). The number of atoms, molecules or ions in a mole of a given substance is 6.02×10^{23}. This value is known as **Avogadro's constant**.

Avogadro's constant = 602 000 000 000 000 000 000 000

For example:

➤ 1 mole of carbon contains 6.02×10^{23} carbon atoms

➤ 1 mole of sulfur dioxide (SO_2) contains 6.02×10^{23} sulfur dioxide molecules.

Moles and relative formula mass

The mass of one mole of a substance in grams is equal to its relative formula mass (M_r).

For example:

➤ The mass of one mole of carbon is 12 g.

➤ The mass of one mole of sulfur dioxide is 64 g.

The number of moles can be calculated using the following formula:

$$\text{moles} = \frac{\text{mass}}{M_r}$$

For example, the number of moles of carbon in 48 g $= \frac{48}{12} = 4$

By rearranging the above equation, the relative formula mass of a compound can be worked out from the number of moles and mass.

Example: Calculate the relative formula mass of the compound given that 0.23 moles has a mass of 36.8 g.

$$M_r = \frac{\text{mass}}{\text{moles}} \qquad M_r = \frac{36.8}{0.23} = 160$$

HT Amounts of substances in equations

Balanced symbol equations give information about the number of moles of reactants and products. For example:

$$2Mg + O_2 \rightarrow 2MgO$$

This equation tells us that 2 moles of magnesium react with one mole of oxygen to form 2 moles of magnesium oxide.

This means that 48 g of Mg (the mass of 2 moles of Mg) reacts with 32 g of oxygen to form 2 moles of magnesium oxide.

	2Mg	+	O_2	→	2MgO
Number of moles reacting	2		1		2
Relative formula mass	24		32		40
Mass reacting/formed (g)	48		32		80

We can use this relationship between mass and moles to calculate reacting masses.

Example: Calculate the mass of magnesium oxide formed when 12 g of magnesium reacts with an excess of oxygen.

	2Mg	+	O_2	→	2MgO
Number of moles reacting	2		1		2
Relative formula mass	24		32		40
Mass reacting/formed (g)	48		32		80
Reacting mass (g)	12				

To get from 48 to 12 we divide by 4

Therefore to find the mass of magnesium oxide formed we divide 80 by 4

The mass of magnesium oxide formed is therefore 20 g.

Empirical formula

The empirical formula is the simplest whole number ratio of each type of atom present in a compound. For example, hexane (C_6H_{12}) has the empirical formula CH_2.

You can work out the empirical formula of a substance from its chemical formula. For example, the empirical formula of ethanoic acid (CH_3COOH) is CH_2O.

The empirical formula of a compound can be calculated from either:
➤ the percentage composition of the compound by mass

or

➤ the mass of each element in the compound.

To calculate the empirical formula:

1. List all the elements in a compound.

2. Divide the data for each element by the relative atomic mass (A_r) of the element (to find the number of moles).

3. Select the smallest answer from step 2 and divide each answer by that result to obtain a ratio.

4. The ratio may need to be scaled up to give whole numbers.

Example 1: What is the empirical formula of a hydrocarbon containing 75% carbon? (Hydrogen = 25%)

	Carbon	:	Hydrogen
	$\frac{75}{12}$	:	$\frac{25}{1}$
	6.25	:	25
÷ 6.25		:		÷ 6.25
	1	:	4

So the empirical formula is C_1H_4 or CH_4.

Example 2: What is the empirical formula of a compound containing 24 g of carbon, 8 g of hydrogen and 32 g of oxygen?

	Carbon	:	Hydrogen		Oxygen
1					
2	$\frac{24}{12}$	:	$\frac{8}{1}$		$\frac{32}{16}$
3 ÷ 2	2	:	8	÷ 2	2	÷ 2
4	1	:	4		1

So the empirical formula is CH_4O.

Molecular formula

The molecular formula is the actual whole number ratio of each type of atom in a compound. It can be the same as the empirical formula or a multiple of the empirical formula. To convert an empirical formula into a molecular formula, you also need to know the relative formula mass of the compound.

Example: A compound has an empirical formula of CH_2 and an M_r of 42. What is its molecular formula?
(A_r for C = 12 and A_r for H = 1)

Work out the relative formula mass of the empirical formula $= 12 + (2 \times 1) = 14$

Then divide the actual M_r by the empirical formula M_r $= \frac{42}{14} = 3$

This gives the multiple.

The molecular formula is C_3H_6.

Percentage yield and atom economy

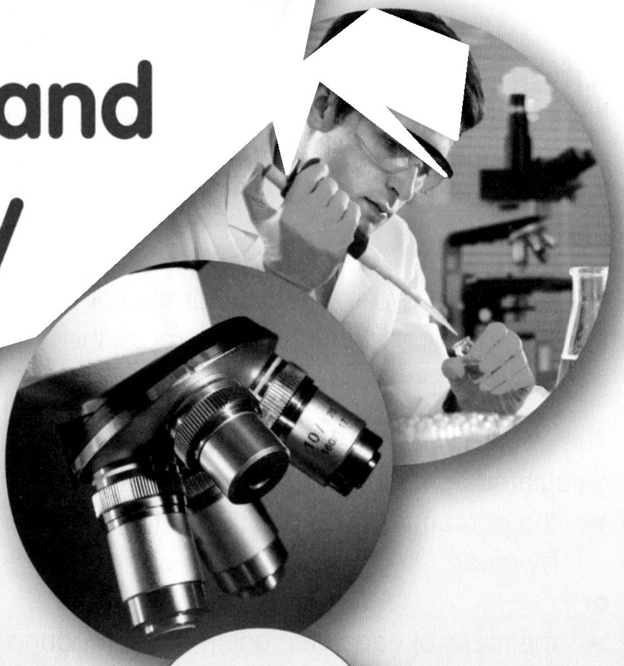

Percentage yield

Balanced symbol equations allow us to work out the mass of products (**yield**) we expect to obtain in a chemical reaction. This is known as the 'theoretical yield'. However, the calculated amount of product may not always be obtained, i.e. the **percentage yield** may not always be 100%.

The actual yield (i.e. the mass of products actually made) compared with the theoretical yield is known as the percentage yield.

$$\% \text{ yield} = \frac{\text{mass of products actually made}}{\text{maximum theoretical mass of product}} \times 100$$

Example: In a chemical reaction the theoretical mass of product is 8.4 g. The mass of product actually obtained was 3.2 g. Calculate the percentage yield for the reaction.

$$\% \text{ yield} = \frac{3.2}{8.4} \times 100 = 38\%$$

The reaction may not go to completion because it is reversible

Reasons why the calculated amount of product is not always obtained

Some of the reactants may react in ways that are different to the expected reaction

Some of the product may be lost when it is separated from the reaction mixture

HT

Example: In the following reaction 12.6 g of nitric acid (HNO_3) reacted with an excess of ammonia (NH_3) to form 12.3 g of ammonium nitrate (NH_4NO_3). Calculate the percentage yield for the reaction.

$$HNO_3 + NH_3 \rightarrow NH_4NO_3$$

Step 1: To calculate the theoretical yield we calculate the expected mass. This is the same calculation as shown on page 30.

The theoretical / expected mass of ammonium nitrate is 16 g.

	NH_3	+ NH_3	$\rightarrow NH_4NO_3$
Number of moles reacting	1	1	1
M_r	63	17	80
Mass reacting / formed in equation (g)	63	÷ 5	80 ÷ 5
Reacting mass (g)	12.6		16

Step 2: Calculate the percentage yield.

$$\% \text{ yield} = \frac{12.3}{16} \times 100$$
$$= 76.9\% \text{ (to 1 d.p.)}$$

Atom economy

Atom economy is a measure of the amount of starting materials that end up as useful products, i.e. a measure of how much starting material is not wasted.

Reactions with a high atom economy are important for sustainable development and are more economic because of the lack of waste formed and the smaller demand for raw materials.

The percentage atom economy of a reaction is calculated from the balanced equation of the reaction and using the following equation:

$$\frac{\text{relative formula mass of desired product from equation}}{\text{sum of relative formula masses of all reactants from equation}} \times 100$$

Keywords

Yield ➤ The amount of product obtained in a reaction

Percentage yield ➤ The ratio of mass of product obtained to mass of product expected

Atom economy ➤ A measure of the amount of starting materials that end up as useful products

Example 1:

Calculate the atom economy for the production of hydrogen from the following reaction.

$$Mg + 2HCl \rightarrow MgCl_2 + H_2$$

In this case, the 'desired product' is hydrogen. Hydrogen has a relative formula mass (M_r) of 2.

Magnesium chloride is the other product in this reaction. Magnesium chloride has an M_r of 95.

The sum of the relative formula masses of the products is 2 + 95 = 97.

Atom economy = $\frac{2}{97} \times 100$

= 2.1% (to 1 d.p.)

Example 2:

Ethene (C_2H_4) can be made by the cracking of decane ($C_{10}H_{22}$) according to the equation:

$$C_{10}H_{22} \rightarrow 2C_2H_4 + C_6H_{14}$$

Calculate the atom economy for this method of producing ethene.

The ratios in the balanced equation need to be taken into account:

M_r ethene = 28

M_r hexane (C_6H_{14}) = 86

We need to multiply by 2 because there is a 2 in front of C_2H_4 in the balanced equation for the reaction

Atom economy = $\frac{2 \times 28}{142} \times 100$

Atom economy = 39.4% (to 1 d.p.)

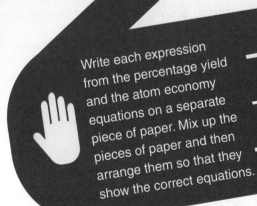

Write each expression from the percentage yield and the atom economy equations on a separate piece of paper. Mix up the pieces of paper and then arrange them so that they show the correct equations.

1. Calculate the percentage yield for a reaction where the actual yield is 3.6g and the expected yield is 5.0 g.
2. Give one reason why the percentage yield for a reaction may not be 100%.
3. Calculate the atom economy for the production of iron in the reaction below.

$$Fe_2O_{3(s)} + 3CO_{(g)} \rightarrow 2Fe_{(l)} + 3CO_{2(g)}$$

Moles, solutions and masses

Concentration of solutions in g/dm³

Many chemical reactions take place in solutions. The concentration of a solution can be measured in mass of **solute** per given volume of solution, e.g. grams per dm³ (1 dm³ = 1000 cm³).

For example, a solution of 5 g/dm³ has 5 g of solute dissolved in 1 dm³ of water. It has half the concentration of a 10 g/dm³ solution of the same solute.

The mass of solute in a solution can be calculated if the concentration and volume of solution are known.

> **Example:** Calculate the mass of solute in 250 cm³ of a solution whose concentration is 8 g/dm³.
>
> **Step 1:** Divide the mass by 1000 (this gives you the mass of solute in 1 cm³).
>
> $$8 \div 1000 = 0.008 \text{ g/cm}^3$$
>
> **Step 2:** Multiply this value by the volume specified.
>
> $$0.008 \times 250 = 2 \text{ g}$$

Concentrations of solutions in mol/dm³

Solution concentrations can also be measured in mol/dm³ (i.e. how many moles of a solute are dissolved in 1 dm³ (1000 cm³) of water).

$$\text{moles} = \frac{\text{mass}}{\text{relative formula mass}}$$

If we know the concentration of a solution in g/dm³, we can work out the concentration in mol/dm³.

> **Example:** What is the concentration in mol/dm³ of a 5 g/dm³ solution of NaOH?
>
> The relative formula mass of NaOH is 40. The number of moles of NaOH present in 5 g is $\frac{5}{40} = 0.125$.
>
> Therefore the concentration is 0.125 mol/dm³.

WS Acid–alkali titrations

A **titration** is an accurate technique that you can use to find out *how much* of an acid is needed to neutralise an alkali of known concentration (called a standard solution).

When neutralisation takes place, the hydrogen ions (H⁺) from the acid join with the hydroxide ions (OH⁻) from the alkali to form water (neutral pH).

> **hydrogen ion + hydroxide ion ⟶ water molecule**
>
> $$H^+_{(aq)} + OH^-_{(aq)} \longrightarrow H_2O_{(l)}$$

Use the following titration method:

1. Wash and rinse a pipette with the alkali that you will use.
2. Use the pipette to measure out a known and accurate volume of the alkali.
3. Place the alkali in a clean, dry conical flask. Add a few drops of a suitable indicator, e.g. phenolphthalein.
4. Place the acid in a burette that has been carefully washed and rinsed with the acid. Take a reading of the volume of acid in the burette (initial reading). Ensure the jet space is filled with acid.
5. Carefully add the acid to the alkali (with swirling of the flask) until the indicator changes colour to show neutrality. This is called the end point. Take a reading of the volume of acid in the burette (final reading).
6. Calculate the volume of acid added (i.e. subtract the initial reading from the final reading).

This method can be repeated to check results.

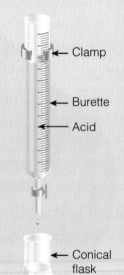

Clamp

Burette

Acid

Conical flask

White tile (allows you to see the colour change clearly)

Alkali and indicator

Titrations can also be used to find the **concentration** of an **acid** or **alkali** providing you know either...

➤ the relative **volumes** of acid and alkali used

or

➤ the **concentration** of the other acid or alkali.

It will help if you break down the calculation.

1 Write down a **balanced equation** for the reaction to determine the ratio of moles of acid to alkali involved.

2 Calculate the number of moles in the solution of known volume and concentration. (You will know the number of moles in the other solution from your previous calculation.)

3 Calculate the concentration of the other solution using this formula:

$$\text{concentration of solution (mol/dm}^3 \text{ or M)} = \frac{\text{number of moles of solute (mol)}}{\text{volume of solution (dm}^3)}$$

Example: A titration is carried out and 0.04 dm³ hydrochloric acid neutralises 0.08 dm³ sodium hydroxide of concentration 1 mol dm⁻³. Calculate the concentration of the hydrochloric acid.

> Write the balanced symbol equation for the reaction

$$HCl_{(aq)} + NaOH_{(aq)} \rightarrow NaCl_{(aq)} + H_2O_{(l)}$$

> You can see that 1 mol of HCl neutralises 1 mol of NaOH

Rearrange the formula:

number of moles of NaOH = concentration of NaOH × volume of NaOH

$$= 1 \text{ mol/dm}^3 \times 0.08 \text{ dm}^3$$
$$= 0.08 \text{ mol}$$

> Number of moles of HCl used up in the reaction is also 0.08 mol

Now calculate the concentration of HCl:

$$\textbf{concentration of HCl} = \frac{\textbf{number of moles of HCl}}{\textbf{volume of HCl}}$$

$$= \frac{0.08 \text{ mol}}{0.04 \text{ dm}^3}$$
$$= 2 \text{ mol/dm}^3$$

Moles and gases

Volumes of gases

The volume of one mole of any gas measured at room temperature and pressure (20°C and 1 atmosphere pressure) is 24 dm³. Based on this fact, equal volumes of gases contain the same number of moles (when compared under the same temperature and pressure).

number of moles of gas = $\dfrac{\text{volume}}{24}$ ← measured in dm³

Example: At 20°C and 1 atmosphere pressure, how many moles are present in 18 dm³ of carbon dioxide gas?

number of moles of gas = $\dfrac{18}{24}$

= 0.75

Gas volumes and equations

The volumes of gaseous reactants and products can be calculated from the balanced equation for the reaction.

Example: Calculate the volume of hydrogen gas formed (at room temperature and pressure) when 3 g of magnesium reacts with excess hydrochloric acid. The equation for the reaction is:

$$Mg_{(s)} + 2HCl_{(aq)} \rightarrow MgCl_{2(aq)} + H_{2(g)}$$

Step 1: Work out the mass of hydrogen formed.

The calculations on page 31 show how to work out the mass of hydrogen formed.

Number of moles reacting	1	2	1	1
Relative formula mass	24	36.5	95	2
Mass reacting / formed in equation (g)	24	73	95	2
Reacting mass (g)	3			

÷8

The mass of hydrogen formed = $\dfrac{2}{8}$ = 0.25 g

Step 2: Work out the number of moles of hydrogen formed.

moles = $\dfrac{\text{mass}}{M_r}$

Therefore the number of moles of hydrogen formed = $\dfrac{0.25}{2}$ = 0.125

Step 3: Work out the volume of hydrogen formed, by rearranging:

number of moles of gas = $\dfrac{\text{volume}}{24}$

We can work out the volume of hydrogen formed.

number of moles × 24 = volume

0.125 × 24 = 3 dm³

Therefore, the volume of hydrogen formed in this experiment is 3 dm³ (3000 cm³).

gases

Using moles to balance equations

The masses of reactants / products in an equation and the M_r values can be used to work out the balancing numbers in a symbol equation.

Example: Balance the equation below given that 8 g of CH_4 reacts with 32 g of oxygen to form 22 g of CO_2 and 18 g of H_2O

$$...CH_4 + ...O_2 \rightarrow ...CO_2 + ...H_2O$$

Chemical	CH_4	O_2	CO_2	H_2O
Mass (from question)	8	32	22	18
M_r	16	32	44	18
Moles = $\dfrac{mass}{M_r}$	$\dfrac{8}{16} = 0.5$	$\dfrac{32}{32} = 1$	$\dfrac{22}{44} = 0.5$	$\dfrac{18}{18} = 1$

We can make this a whole number ratio by dividing all answers by the smallest answer

÷ 0.5		$\dfrac{0.5}{0.5} = 1$	$\dfrac{1}{0.5} = 2$	$\dfrac{0.5}{0.5} = 1$	$\dfrac{1}{0.5} = 2$

The balanced equation is therefore:

$$.......CH_4 + ..2...O_2 \rightarrow ....CO_2 + ..2...H_2O$$

Collect 73 empty 330 ml drinks cans.
You will be able to picture the volume of one mole of gas at room temperature and pressure.
Actually this is slightly more than one mole but only by approximately a quarter of one can!

1. At 20 °C and 1 atmosphere pressure, how many moles are present in 1.5 dm³ of neon gas?
2. Calculate the volume of carbon dioxide gas formed (at room temperature and pressure) when 40 g of calcium carbonate reacts with excess hydrochloric acid. The equation for the reaction is shown below.

$$CaCO_{3(s)} + 2HCl_{(aq)} \rightarrow CaCl_{2(aq)} + H_2O_{(l)} + CO_{2(g)}$$

3. Balance the equation below for the reaction that occurs when 7 g of silicon reacts with 35.5 g of chlorine to form 42.5 g of silicon chloride.

$$..........Si + ...Cl_2 \rightarrow ....SiCl_4$$

Mind map

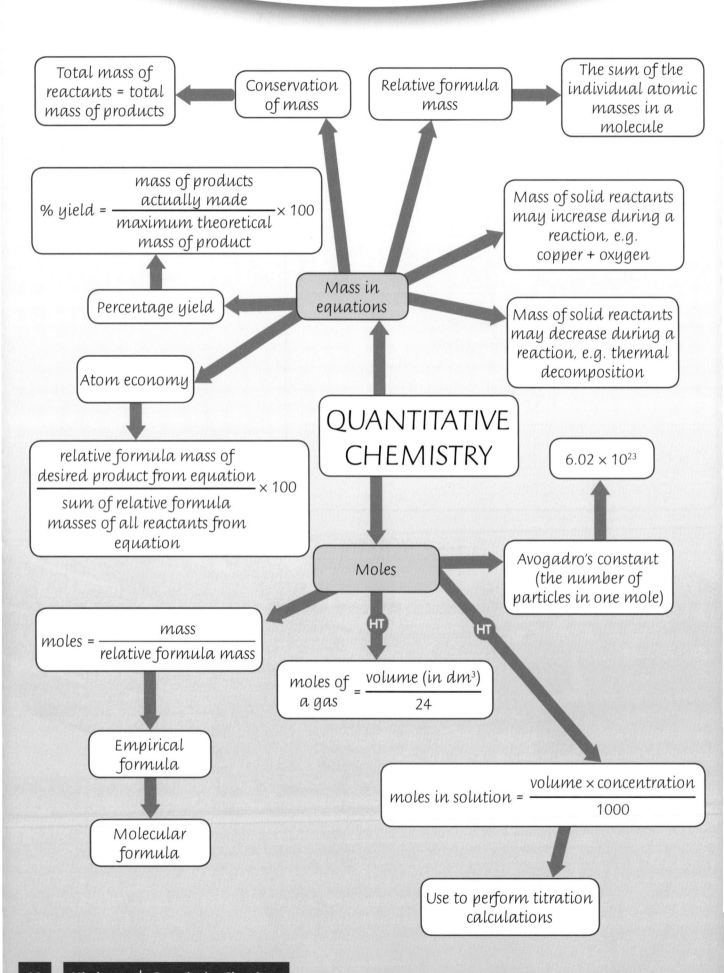

Total mass of reactants = total mass of products

Conservation of mass

Relative formula mass

The sum of the individual atomic masses in a molecule

$$\% \text{ yield} = \frac{\text{mass of products actually made}}{\text{maximum theoretical mass of product}} \times 100$$

Mass of solid reactants may increase during a reaction, e.g. copper + oxygen

Percentage yield

Mass in equations

Mass of solid reactants may decrease during a reaction, e.g. thermal decomposition

Atom economy

QUANTITATIVE CHEMISTRY

6.02×10^{23}

$$\frac{\text{relative formula mass of desired product from equation}}{\text{sum of relative formula masses of all reactants from equation}} \times 100$$

Avogadro's constant (the number of particles in one mole)

Moles

$$\text{moles} = \frac{\text{mass}}{\text{relative formula mass}}$$

HT

$$\text{moles of a gas} = \frac{\text{volume (in dm}^3\text{)}}{24}$$

HT

$$\text{moles in solution} = \frac{\text{volume} \times \text{concentration}}{1000}$$

Empirical formula

Molecular formula

Use to perform titration calculations

Practice questions

1. Calcium carbonate thermally decomposes when heated to form calcium oxide and carbon dioxide gas.

   The equation for the reaction is shown below.

   $$CaCO_{3(s)} \rightarrow CaO_{(s)} + CO_{2(g)}$$

   In an experiment, a student placed 10 g of $CaCO_3$ in a crucible and heated it strongly for 10 minutes.

   a) Will the mass of solid in the crucible at the end of the experiment be higher or lower than 10 g? Explain your answer.   **(2 marks)**

   b) With reference to the periodic table (see page 104), what is the relative formula mass of calcium carbonate?   **(1 mark)**

   c) Calculate the mass of carbon dioxide that would be produced in this experiment.   **(2 marks)**

   In another experiment, the student investigated the reaction of magnesium with oxygen.

   The equation for the reaction is shown below.

   $$2Mg_{(s)} + O_{2(g)} \rightarrow 2\,MgO_{(s)}$$

   The student heated 0.15 g of magnesium and at the end of the experiment she had made 0.20 g of magnesium oxide.

   d) How many atoms of magnesium are there in 0.15 g of magnesium? (Avogadro's constant is 6×10^{23})   **(2 marks)**

   e) The teacher said that 0.25 g of magnesium oxide was expected to have been made in this experiment.

       Calculate the percentage yield.   **(1 mark)**

2. During a titration, 22.50 cm³ of 0.20 mol/dm³ hydrochloric acid neutralised 25.00 cm³ of sodium hydroxide solution.

   The equation for the reaction is shown below.

   $$NaOH_{(aq)} + HCl_{(aq)} \rightarrow NaCl_{(aq)} + H_2O_{(l)}$$

   a) How many moles are present in 22.50 cm³ of 0.20 mol/dm³ hydrochloric acid?   **(1 mark)**

   b) How many moles of sodium hydroxide were present in the 25.00 cm³ of sodium hydroxide? Explain your answer.   **(2 marks)**

   c) Calculate the concentration of the sodium hydroxide solution in mol/dm³.   **(2 marks)**

   d) Calculate the concentration of the sodium hydroxide solution in g/dm³.   **(2 marks)**

Reactivity of metals and metal extraction

r the gain
electrons

Reaction of metals with oxygen

Many metals react with oxygen to form metal oxides, for example:

> copper + oxygen ⟶ copper oxide

These reactions are called **oxidation** reactions. Oxidation reactions take place when a chemical gains oxygen.

When a substance loses oxygen it is called a **reduction** reaction.

The reactivity series

When metals react they form positive ions. The more easily the metal forms a positive ion the more reactive the metal.

Calcium and magnesium are both in group 2 of the periodic table so will form 2+ ions when they react. Calcium is more reactive than magnesium so it has a greater tendency/is more likely to form the 2+ ion.

Decreasing reactivity

Metal	Reaction with water	Reaction with acid
Potassium	Very vigorous	Explosive
Sodium	Vigorous	Dangerous
Lithium	Steady	Very vigorous
Calcium	Steady fizzing and bubbling	Vigorous
Magnesium	Slow reaction	Steady fizzing and bubbling
Aluminium	Slow reaction	Steady fizzing and bubbling
*Carbon		
Zinc	Very slow reaction	Gentle fizzing and bubbling
Iron	Extremely slow	Slight fizzing and bubbling
*Hydrogen		
Copper	No reaction	No reaction
Silver	No reaction	No reaction
Gold	No reaction	No reaction

* included for comparison

The reactivity series can also be used to predict displacement reactions.

> zinc + copper oxide ⟶ zinc oxide + copper

In this reaction…
➤ zinc displaces (i.e. takes the place of) copper
➤ zinc is oxidised (i.e. it gains oxygen)
➤ copper oxide is reduced (i.e. it loses oxygen).

Gold

Extraction of metals and reduction

Unreactive metals, such as gold, are found in the Earth's crust as pure metals. Most metals are found as compounds and chemical reactions are required to extract the metal. The method of extraction depends on the position of the metal in the reactivity series.

Position of metal in the reactivity series

above carbon → metal extracted by electrolysis

below carbon → metal extracted by reduction with carbon

For example, iron is found in the earth as iron(III) oxide, Fe_2O_3. The iron(III) oxide can be reduced by reacting it with carbon.

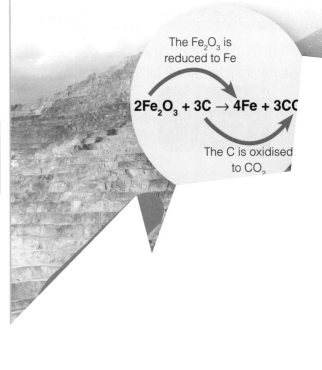
The Fe_2O_3 is reduced to Fe

$$2Fe_2O_3 + 3C \rightarrow 4Fe + 3CO_2$$

The C is oxidised to CO_2

HT Oxidation and reduction in terms of electrons

Oxidation and reduction can also be defined in terms of electrons:

O oxidation
I is
L loss (of electrons)
R reduction
I is
G gain (of electrons)

This mnemonic can be useful to work out what is being oxidised and reduced in displacement reactions, for example:

magnesium +	copper sulfate	→	magnesium sulfate	+ copper
Mg	+ CuSO₄	→	MgSO₄	+ Cu

The ionic equation for this reaction is:

Mg **loses electrons** to become Mg²⁺

Oxidation

$$Mg + Cu^{2+} \rightarrow Mg^{2+} + Cu$$

Reduction

Cu²⁺ **gains electrons** to become Cu

1. Write a word equation for t
2. Both sodium and lithium react t
   tendency/is more likely t
3. Name two metals from the reactiv
HT 4. In the equation below, whic

Reactions of acids

Reactions of acids with metals

Acids react with metals that are above hydrogen in the reactivity series to make **salts** and hydrogen, for example:

magnesium + hydrochloric acid → magnesium chloride + hydrogen

This is a salt

The reactions of metals with acids are **redox** reactions. The ionic equation for the reaction of magnesium with hydrochloric acid is:

$$Mg + 2H^+ \rightarrow Mg^{2+} + H_2$$

The metal (in this case magnesium) is oxidised, i.e. it loses electrons.

The hydrogen ions are reduced, i.e. they gain electrons.

Mg is **oxidised**, i.e. it loses electrons (to form Mg^{2+})

$$Mg + 2H^+ \rightarrow Mg^{2+} + H_2$$

H^+ is **reduced**, i.e. it gains electrons (to form H_2)

Neutralisation of acids and the preparation of salts

Acids can be neutralised by the following reactions.

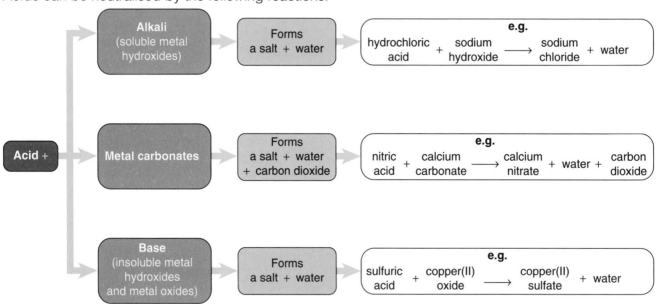

Acid +

Alkali (soluble metal hydroxides) → Forms a salt + water → **e.g.** hydrochloric acid + sodium hydroxide → sodium chloride + water

Metal carbonates → Forms a salt + water + carbon dioxide → **e.g.** nitric acid + calcium carbonate → calcium nitrate + water + carbon dioxide

Base (insoluble metal hydroxides and metal oxides) → Forms a salt + water → **e.g.** sulfuric acid + copper(II) oxide → copper(II) sulfate + water

The first part of the salt formed contains the positive ion (usually the metal) from the alkali, base or carbonate followed by...

➤ chloride if hydrochloric acid was used
➤ sulfate if sulfuric acid was used
➤ nitrate if nitric acid was used.

For example, when calcium hydroxide is reacted with sulfuric acid, the salt formed is calcium sulfate.

Write examples of neutralisation reactions on pieces of paper or card. Stick them on a wall near where you study, so that you regularly see them.

Making salts

Salts can be either soluble or insoluble. The majority of salts are soluble.

The general rules for deciding whether a salt will be soluble are as follows.

➤ All common sodium, potassium and ammonium salts are soluble.
➤ All nitrates are soluble.
➤ All common chlorides, except silver chloride, are soluble.
➤ All common sulfates, except barium and calcium, are soluble.
➤ All common carbonates are insoluble, except potassium, sodium and ammonium.

Keywords

Salt ➤ A product of the reaction that occurs when an acid is neutralised

HT **Redox** ➤ A reaction in which both oxidation and reduction occur

Crystallisation ➤ A method used to separate a soluble solid from its solution when you want to collect the solid

Preparation of soluble salts

Soluble salts can be prepared by the following method.

| Add solid to the acid until no more reacts | Filter off the excess solid | Obtain the solid salt by **crystallisation** |

For example, copper(II) sulfate crystals can be made by reacting copper(II) oxide with sulfuric acid.

Copper(II) oxide

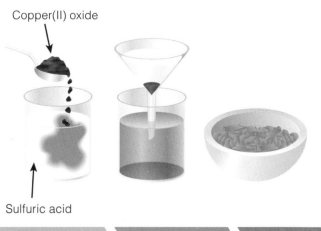

Sulfuric acid

Copper(II) sulfate

| Add copper(II) oxide to sulfuric acid | Filter to remove any unreacted copper(II) oxide | Evaporate to leave behind blue crystals of the 'salt' copper(II) sulfate |

1. Write a word equation for the reaction that occurs when zinc reacts with sulfuric acid.
HT 2. Identify the species that is oxidised in the following reaction.

$$Fe + 2H^+ \longrightarrow Fe^{2+} + H_2$$

3. Other than an alkali, name a substance that can neutralise an acid.
4. Name the salt formed when lithium oxide reacts with nitric acid.
5. What are the three main steps in preparing a soluble salt from an acid and a metal oxide?
6. Which one of the following salts is insoluble?

ammonium carbonate
barium sulfate
copper(II) nitrate

pH, neutralisation, acid strength and electrolysis

Indicators, the pH scale and neutralisation reactions

Indicators are useful dyes that become different colours in acids and alkalis.

Indicator	Colour in acid	Colour in alkali
Litmus	Red	Blue
Phenolphthalein	Colourless	Pink
Methyl orange	Pink	Yellow

The pH scale measures the acidity or alkalinity of a solution. The pH scale runs from 0 to 14 and the pH of a solution can be measured using universal indicator or a pH probe.

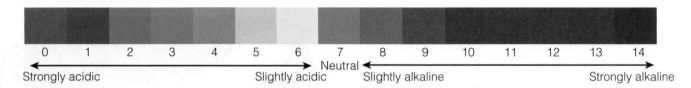

| 0 | 1 | 2 | 3 | 4 | 5 | 6 | 7 | 8 | 9 | 10 | 11 | 12 | 13 | 14 |

Neutral

Strongly acidic   Slightly acidic Slightly alkaline   Strongly alkaline

Acids are solutions that contain hydrogen ions (H^+). The higher the concentration of hydrogen ions, the more acidic the solution (i.e. the lower the pH).

Alkalis are solutions that contain hydroxide ions (OH^-). The higher the concentration of hydroxide ions, the more alkaline the solution (i.e. the higher the pH).

When an acid is neutralised by an alkali, the hydrogen ions from the acid react with the hydroxide ions in the alkali to form water.

$$H^+_{(aq)} + OH^-_{(aq)} \rightarrow H_2O_{(l)}$$

HT **Strong acids**, such as hydrochloric, sulfuric and nitric acids, are those that completely ionise in aqueous solution. For example:

$$HCl_{(aq)} \rightarrow H^+_{(aq)} + Cl^-_{(aq)}$$

This means dissolved in water

Weak acids, such as ethanoic, citric and carbonic acids, only partially ionise in water. For example:

$$CH_3COOH_{(aq)} \rightleftharpoons CH_3COO^-_{(aq)} + H^+_{(aq)}$$

This sign means that the reaction is reversible, i.e. that the acid does not fully ionise

The pH of an acid is a measure of the concentration of hydrogen ions. When two different acids of the same concentration have different pH values the strongest acid will have the lowest pH.

The pH scale is a logarithmic scale. As the pH decreases by 1 unit (e.g. from 3 to 2) the hydrogen ion concentration increases by a factor of 10.

Electrolysis

An electric current is the flow of electrons through a conductor but it can also flow by the movement of ions through a solution or a liquid.

Covalent compounds do not contain free electrons or ions that can move. So they will not conduct electricity when solid, liquid, gas or in solution.

The ions in:

➤ an **ionic solid** are fixed and cannot move
➤ an **ionic substance** that is **molten** or in **solution** are free to move.

Electrolysis is a chemical reaction that involves passing electricity through an **electrolyte**. An electrolyte is a liquid that conducts electricity. Electrolytes are either molten ionic compounds or solutions of ionic compounds. Electrolytes are decomposed during electrolysis.

➤ The positive ions (**cations**) move to, and discharge at, the negative electrode (**cathode**).
➤ The negative ions (**anions**) move to, and discharge at, the positive electrode (**anode**).

Electrons are removed from the anions at the anode. These electrons then flow around the circuit to the cathode and are transferred to the cations.

HT Strong acid ➤ An acid that fully ionises when dissolved

HT Weak acid ➤ An acid that partially ionises when dissolved in water

Electrolyte ➤ A liquid or solution containing ions that is broken down during electrolysis

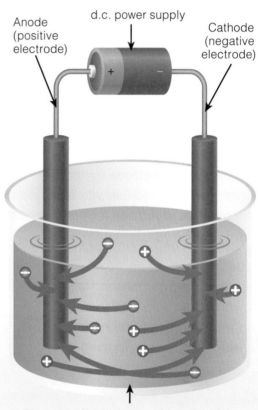

Anode (positive electrode)

d.c. power supply

Cathode (negative electrode)

Electrolyte (liquid that conducts electricity and decomposes in electrolysis)

of paper in
on the pH scale.
back of each, write the
pH num   that each colour
corresponds to.
Mix up the pieces of paper,
then practise putting them into

Applications of electrolysis

Electrolysis of molten ionic compounds

When an ionic compound melts, electrostatic forces between the charged ions in the crystal lattice are broken down, meaning that the ions are free to move.

When a direct current is passed through a molten ionic compound:

➤ positively charged ions are attracted towards the **negative electrode** (cathode)
➤ negatively charged ions are attracted towards the **positive electrode** (anode).

For example, in the electrolysis of molten lead bromide:

➤ positively charged lead ions are attracted towards the **cathode**, forming lead
➤ negatively charged bromide ions are attracted towards the **anode**, forming bromine.

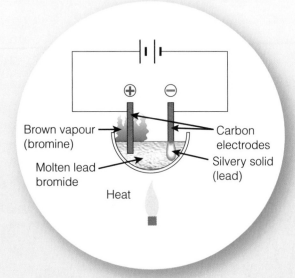

Brown vapour (bromine)
Carbon electrodes
Molten lead bromide
Silvery solid (lead)
Heat

When ions get to the oppositely charged electrode they are **discharged** – they lose their charge. For example, in the electrolysis of molten lead bromide, the non-metal ion loses electrons to the positive electrode to form a bromine atom. The bromine atom then bonds with a second atom to form a bromine molecule.

(ws) Using electrolysis to extract metals

Aluminium is the most abundant metal in the Earth's crust. It must be obtained from its ore by electrolysis because it is too reactive to be extracted by heating with carbon. The electrodes are made of graphite (a type of carbon). The aluminium ore (bauxite) is purified to leave aluminium oxide, which is then melted so that the ions can move. Cryolite is added to increase the conductivity and lower the melting point.

When a current passes through the molten mixture:

➤ positively charged aluminium ions move towards the negative electrode (**cathode**) and form aluminium
➤ negatively charged oxygen ions move towards the positive electrode (**anode**) and form oxygen.

The positive electrodes gradually wear away (because the graphite electrodes react with the oxygen to form carbon dioxide gas). This means they have to be replaced every so often. Extracting aluminium can be quite an expensive process because of the cost of the large amounts of electrical energy needed to carry it out.

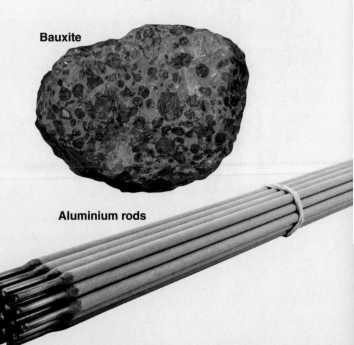

Bauxite

Aluminium rods

Electrolysis of aqueous solutions

When a solution undergoes electrolysis, there is also water present. During electrolysis water molecules break down into hydrogen ions and hydroxide ions.

$$H_2O_{(l)} \rightarrow H^+_{(aq)} + OH^-_{(aq)}$$

This means that when an aqueous compound is electrolysed there are two cations present (H^+ from water and the metal cation from the compound) and two anions present (OH^- from water and the anion from the compound).

Solution	Product at cathode	Product at anode
copper chloride	copper	chlorine
sodium sulfate	hydrogen	oxygen
water (diluted with sulfuric acid to aid conductivity)	hydrogen	oxygen

For example, in copper(II) sulfate solution…
➤ cations present: Cu^{2+} and H^+
➤ anions present: SO_4^{2-} and OH^-

At the positive electrode (anode): *Oxygen is produced unless the solution contains halide ions*. In this case the oxygen is produced.

At the negative electrode (cathode): *The least reactive element is formed*. The reactivity series in Module 16 will be helpful here. In this case, hydrogen is formed.

HT Half-equations

During electrolysis, the cation that is discharged at the cathode gains electrons (is reduced) to form the element. For example:

$$Cu^{2+} + 2e^- \rightarrow Cu$$

$$2H^+ + 2e^- \rightarrow H_2$$

At the anode the anion loses electrons (is oxidised). For example:

$$2Cl^- \rightarrow Cl_2 + 2e^-$$

this can also be written as $2Cl^- - 2e^- \rightarrow Cl_2$

$$4OH^- \rightarrow O_2 + 2H_2O + 4e^-$$

or $4OH^- - 4e^- \rightarrow O_2 + 2H_2O$

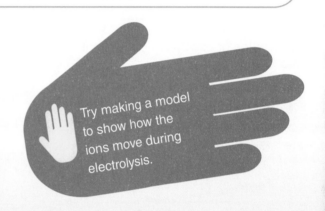

Try making a model to show how the ions move during electrolysis.

Example:

What are the three products of the electrolysis of sodium chloride solution?

Cations present: Na^+ and H^+
Q. What happens at the cathode?
A. Hydrogen is less reactive than sodium therefore hydrogen gas is formed.

Anions present: Cl^- and OH^-
Q. What happens at the anode?
A. A halide ion (Cl^-) is present therefore chlorine will be formed.

The sodium ions and hydroxide ions stay in solution (i.e. sodium hydroxide solution remains).

WS **How aqueous solutions can be electrolysed in the laboratory**

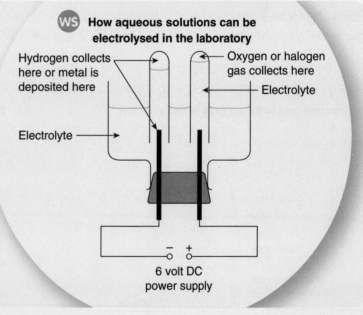

Hydrogen collects here or metal is deposited here

Oxygen or halogen gas collects here

Electrolyte

Electrolyte

6 volt DC power supply

Energy changes in reactions

Exothermic and endothermic reactions

Energy is not created or destroyed during chemical reactions, i.e. the amount of energy in the universe at the end of a chemical reaction is the same as before the reaction takes place.

Type of reaction	Is energy given out or taken in?	What happens to the temperature of the surroundings?
Exothermic	out	increases
Endothermic	in	decreases

Examples of **exothermic** reactions include...
> combustion
> neutralisation
> many oxidation reactions
> precipitation reactions
> displacement reactions.

Everyday applications of exothermic reactions include self-heating cans and hand warmers.

Examples of **endothermic** reactions include...
> thermal decomposition
> the reaction between citric acid and sodium hydrogen carbonate.

Some changes, such as dissolving salts in water, can be either exothermic or endothermic. Some sports injury packs are based on endothermic reactions.

Reaction profiles

For a chemical reaction to occur, the reacting particles must collide together with sufficient energy. The minimum amount of energy that the particles must have in order to react is known as the 'activation energy'.

Reaction profiles can be used to show the relative energies of reactants and products, the activation energy and the overall energy change of a reaction.

Reaction profile for an exothermic reaction

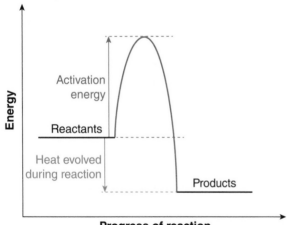

Reaction profile for an endothermic reaction

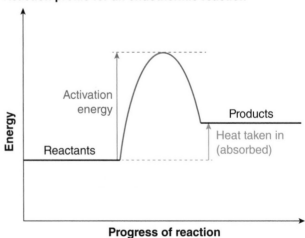

Chemical reactions in which more energy is made when new bonds are made than was used to break the existing bonds are **exothermic**.

Chemical reactions in which more energy is used to break the existing bonds than is released in making the new bonds are **endothermic**.

The energy change of reactions

During a chemical reaction:

➤ bonds are broken in the reactant molecules – this is an endothermic process

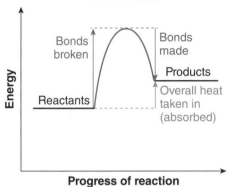

Endothermic

➤ bonds are made to form the product molecules – this is an exothermic process.

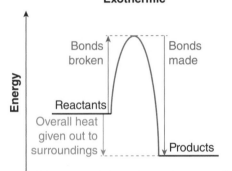

Exothermic

Example:

Hydrogen is burned in oxygen to produce water:

$$hydrogen + oxygen \rightarrow water$$

$$2H_{2(g)} + O_{2(g)} \rightarrow 2H_2O_{(l)}$$

$$2H-H + O=O \rightarrow 2H-O-H$$

The following are **bond energies** for the **reactants** and **products**:

H–H is 436 kJ   O=O is 496 kJ   O–H is 463 kJ

Calculate the energy change.

You can calculate the energy change using this method:

1 Calculate the energy used to break bonds:

$$(2 \times H-H) + O=O = (2 \times 436) + 496 = \textbf{1368 kJ}$$

2 Calculate the energy released when new bonds are made:

(Water is made up of 2 × O–H bonds.)
$$2 \times H-O-H = 2 \times (2 \times 463) = \textbf{1852 kJ}$$

Enthalpy change (ΔH) = energy used to break bonds – energy released when new bonds are made

$$\Delta H = 1368 - 1852$$
$$\Delta H = \textbf{-484 kJ}$$

The reaction is **exothermic** because the energy from making the bonds is **more than** the energy needed to break the bonds.

Pull apart 'things' that are 'bonded' together, such as a pen from its lid. You have to use energy to separate the pen from the lid just like you have to use energy to break chemical 'things' that are 'bonded' together!

1. What happens to the temperature of the surroundings when an endothermic reaction takes place?
2. Draw and label a reaction profile for an exothermic reaction.
3. The energy required to break the bonds in a reaction is 2314 kJ. The energy released when the new bonds are made is 3613 kJ. What is the energy change for this reaction?
4. Is the reaction in question 3 exothermic or endothermic? Explain your answer.

Chemical cells and fuel cells

Keywords

Chemical cell ➤ A system containing chemicals that react together to produce electricity
Battery ➤ A combination of cells connected in series
Fuel cell ➤ A chemical cell where the source of fuel is supplied externally

Cells and batteries

Cells contain chemicals which react to produce electricity. A typical cell consists of two different metals in contact with an electrolyte.

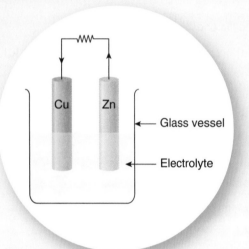

Everyday chemical 'cells'

Electricity flows from the more reactive metal to the less reactive metal. In the above case, electricity would flow through the wire from the zinc to the copper.

The voltage produced by a cell depends upon many factors including…

➤ the type of metal used as the electrode
➤ the chemical used as the electrolyte.

A battery consists of two or more chemical cells connected together in series to provide a greater voltage.

In non-rechargeable cells and batteries, such as alkaline batteries, when one of the reactants has been used up the chemical reactions stop, meaning that electricity is no longer produced.

Look at old batteries in your home. Can you see what chemicals they contain?

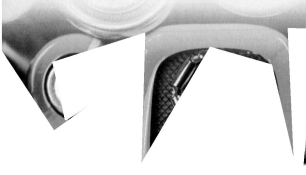

Fuel cells

Fuel cells differ from cells in that they are supplied by an external source of fuel, for example, hydrogen together with oxygen or air. The fuel is oxidised electrochemically within the cell to produce a potential difference.

The diagram on the right shows a simple fuel cell.

The overall reaction in a hydrogen fuel cell (a fuel cell where hydrogen is the fuel) involves the oxidation of hydrogen to produce water.

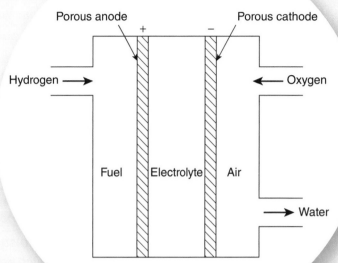

$$2H_{2(g)} + O_{2(g)} \rightarrow 2H_2O_{(g)}$$

As water is the only waste product, fuel cells can be said to be more environmentally friendly than some other sources of energy (such as fossil fuels), which produce carbon dioxide.

Fuel cells, provided that they are constantly supplied with fuel and oxygen, do not run out in the same way that alkaline batteries do and while they are limited in their use they represent a potential alternative to rechargeable cells and batteries.

Hydrogen fuel cell

HT **Half-equations for the reactions taking place in the hydrogen fuel cell**

Where hydrogen is the fuel used in a fuel cell, the following reactions take place at the electrodes.

Anode: $H_{2(g)} \rightarrow 2H^+_{(aq)} + 2e^-$

Cathode: $4H^+_{(aq)} + O_{2(g)} + 4e^- \rightarrow 2H_2O_{(g)}$

Hydrogen Station

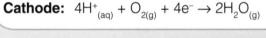

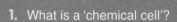

1. What is a 'chemical cell'?
2. What is the main difference between a fuel cell and a chemical cell?
3. What is the waste product from a hydrogen fuel cell?
4. Write the half-equation for the reaction that takes place at the cathode of a hydrogen fuel cell.

Mind map

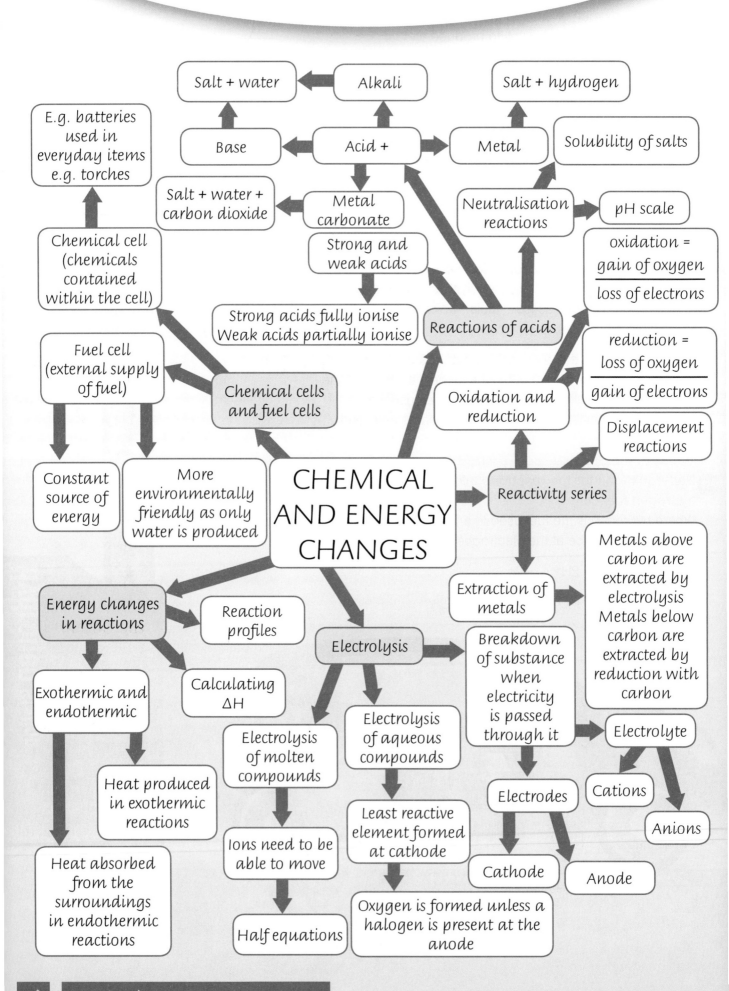

Salt + water

Alkali

Salt + hydrogen

E.g. batteries used in everyday items e.g. torches

Base

Acid +

Metal

Solubility of salts

Salt + water + carbon dioxide

Metal carbonate

Neutralisation reactions

pH scale

Chemical cell (chemicals contained within the cell)

Strong and weak acids

oxidation = gain of oxygen / loss of electrons

Fuel cell (external supply of fuel)

Strong acids fully ionise Weak acids partially ionise

Reactions of acids

reduction = loss of oxygen / gain of electrons

Chemical cells and fuel cells

Oxidation and reduction

Displacement reactions

Constant source of energy

More environmentally friendly as only water is produced

CHEMICAL AND ENERGY CHANGES

Reactivity series

Energy changes in reactions

Reaction profiles

Extraction of metals

Metals above carbon are extracted by electrolysis Metals below carbon are extracted by reduction with carbon

Exothermic and endothermic

Calculating ΔH

Electrolysis

Breakdown of substance when electricity is passed through it

Electrolyte

Heat produced in exothermic reactions

Electrolysis of molten compounds

Electrolysis of aqueous compounds

Electrodes

Cations

Heat absorbed from the surroundings in endothermic reactions

Ions need to be able to move

Least reactive element formed at cathode

Cathode

Anode

Anions

Half equations

Oxygen is formed unless a halogen is present at the anode

Practice questions

1. Zinc is found in the Earth's crust as zinc oxide.

   a) Write a balanced symbol equation for the reaction between zinc and oxygen to form zinc oxide. **(1 mark)**

   b) Zinc can be extracted by reacting the zinc oxide with magnesium, as shown in the equation below.

   $Mg + ZnO \rightarrow MgO + Zn$

   Which species has been reduced in this reaction?
   Explain your answer. **(2 marks)**

   c) Is zinc more or less reactive than magnesium?
   Explain your answer with reference to the above equation. **(2 marks)**

   d) Would you expect zinc metal to normally be extracted from its ore by electrolysis or by reduction with carbon? Explain your answer. **(2 marks)**

   e) Zinc will react with copper solutions according to the ionic equation below.

   $Zn_{(s)} + Cu^{2+}_{(aq)} \rightarrow Zn^{2+}_{(aq)} + Cu_{(s)}$

   Which species is oxidised in this reaction?
   Explain your answer. **(2 marks)**

2. In a methane fuel cell the equation for the overall reaction is:

$$\begin{array}{c} H \\ | \\ H-C-H \\ | \\ H \end{array} + 2\,O{=}O \rightarrow O{=}C{=}O + 2\,H{-}O{-}H$$

   a) What is a fuel cell? **(1 mark)**

   b) What is the main difference between a fuel cell and a chemical cell? **(1 mark)**

   c) The reaction between methane and oxygen is exothermic. Draw and label a reaction profile for this reaction. **(3 marks)**

   d) Use the bond energy values in the table below to calculate the value of ΔH for the reaction between methane and oxygen. **(3 marks)**

Bond	Energy kJ/mol
C–H	413
O=O	498
C=O	805
O–H	464

Rates of reaction

22

Calculating rates of reactions

The **rate** of a chemical reaction can be determined by measuring the quantity of a reactant used or (more commonly) the quantity of a product formed over time.

$$\text{mean rate of reaction} = \frac{\text{quantity of reactant used}}{\text{time taken}}$$

$$\text{mean rate of reaction} = \frac{\text{quantity of product formed}}{\text{time taken}}$$

For example, if 46 cm³ of gas is produced in 23 seconds then the mean rate of reaction is 2 cm³/s.

HT Rates of reaction can also be determined from graphs.

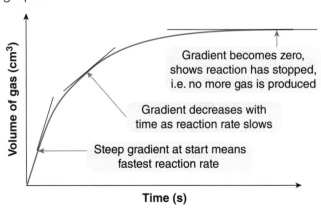

Gradient becomes zero, shows reaction has stopped, i.e. no more gas is produced

Gradient decreases with time as reaction rate slows

Steep gradient at start means fastest reaction rate

If the gradient of the tangent is calculated, this gives a numerical measure of the rate of reaction.
For example:

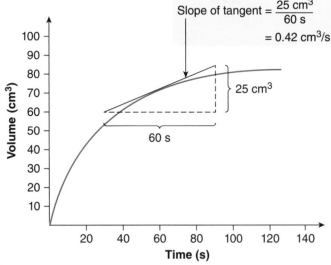

Slope of tangent = $\frac{25 \text{ cm}^3}{60 \text{ s}}$ = 0.42 cm³/s

Keywords

Rate ➤ A measure of the speed of a chemical reaction
Catalyst ➤ A species that alters the rate of a reaction without being used up or chemically changed at the end

Factors affecting the rates of reactions

There are five factors that affect the rate of chemical reactions:

➤ concentrations of the reactants in solution
➤ pressure of reacting gases
➤ surface area of any solid reactants
➤ temperature
➤ presence of a catalyst.

During experiments the rate of a chemical reaction can be found by...

➤ measuring the mass of the reaction mixture (e.g. if a gas is lost during a reaction)
➤ measuring the volume of gas produced
➤ observing a solution becoming opaque or changing colour.

Weighing the reaction mixture

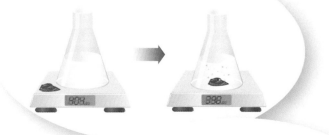

Measuring the volume of gas produced

Observing the formation of a precipitate

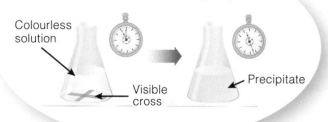

Colourless solution

Visible cross

Precipitate

| As particle size decreases | The surface area to volume ratio increases | and the rate of reaction increases |

Add a teaspoon of sugar to a cup of tea or coffee and stir.
Time how long it takes for the sugar to dissolve.
Occasionally, lift the teaspoon to check that the sugar has all dissolved.
Make another cup of tea or coffee and repeat the experiment but using a cube of sugar instead.
Does sugar dissolve more quickly as a cube or as individual granules?
Dissolving is a physical process rather than a chemical reaction but the principle is the same!

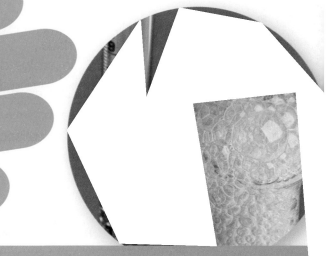

1. What is the rate of the reaction in which 12 g of reactant is used up over 16 seconds?
2. State two factors that affect the rate of reaction.
3. How would you measure the rate of a reaction where one of the products is hydrogen gas?
4. What is the effect on the rate of a reaction as the surface area to volume ratio of a solid reactant increases?

Collision theory, activation energy and catalysts

23

Factors affecting rates of reaction

Collision theory explains how various factors affect rates of reaction.

It states that, for a chemical reaction to occur…

1 The reactant particles must collide with each other.   **AND**   **2** They must collide with sufficient energy – this amount of energy is known as the **activation energy**.

Surface area	Temperature	Pressure	Concentration
			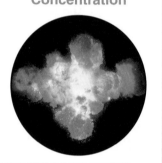
A smaller particle size means a higher surface area to volume ratio. With smaller particles, more collisions can take place, meaning a greater rate of reaction.	Increasing the temperature increases the rate of reaction because the particles are moving more quickly and so will collide more often. Also, more particles will possess the activation energy, so a greater proportion of collisions will result in a reaction.	At a higher pressure, the gas particles are closer together, so there is a greater chance of them colliding, resulting in a higher rate of reaction.	At a higher concentration, there are more reactant particles in the same volume of solution, which increases the chance of collisions and increases the rate of reaction.
Large pieces – small surface area to volume ratio **Small pieces** – large surface area to volume ratio	**Low temperature** **High temperature** 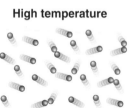	**Low pressure** **High pressure** 	**Low concentration** **High concentration** 

Enzyme (biological catalyst)

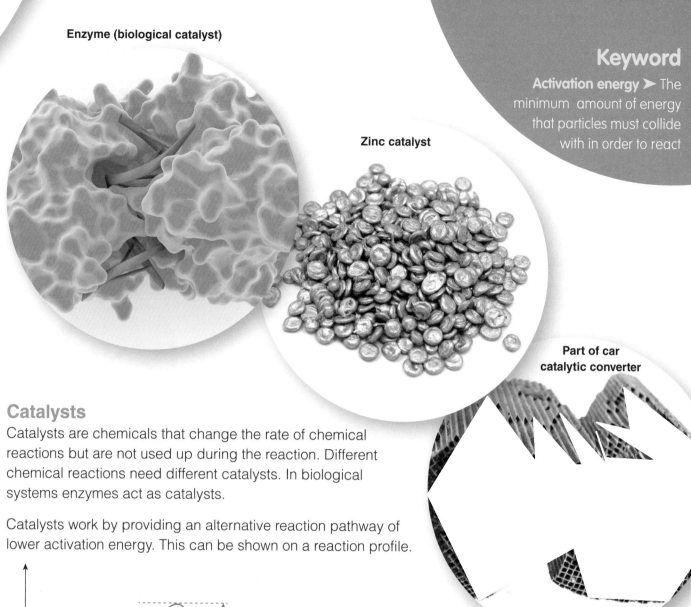

Activation energy ➤ The minimum amount of energy that particles must collide with in order to react

Zinc catalyst

Part of car catalytic converter

Catalysts

Catalysts are chemicals that change the rate of chemical reactions but are not used up during the reaction. Different chemical reactions need different catalysts. In biological systems enzymes act as catalysts.

Catalysts work by providing an alternative reaction pathway of lower activation energy. This can be shown on a reaction profile.

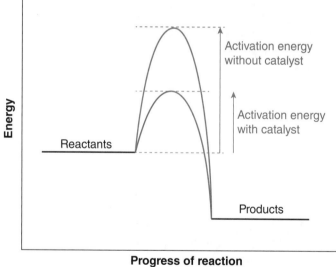

Activation energy without catalyst

Activation energy with catalyst

Reactants

Products

Energy (y-axis)

Progress of reaction (x-axis)

Catalysts are not reactants and so they are not included in the chemical equation.

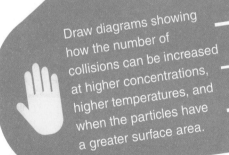

Draw diagrams showing how the number of collisions can be increased at higher concentrations, higher temperatures, and when the particles have a greater surface area.

1. What is collision theory?
2. What is meant by the term 'activation energy'?
3. Why does a higher concentration of solution increase the rate of a chemical reaction?
4. What is a catalyst?
5. Explain how catalysts increase the rate of chemical reactions.

Reversible reactions and equilibrium

24

Reversible reactions

In some reactions, the products of the reaction can react to produce the original reactants. These reactions are called reversible reactions. For example:

➤ Heating ammonium chloride:

$$NH_4Cl_{(s)} \rightleftharpoons NH_{3(g)} + HCl_{(g)}$$

we use this symbol to represent a reversible reaction

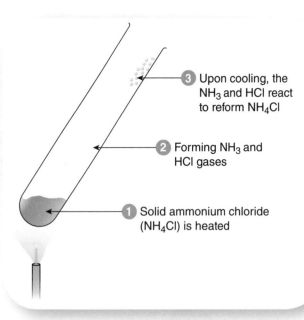

3 Upon cooling, the NH_3 and HCl react to reform NH_4Cl

2 Forming NH_3 and HCl gases

1 Solid ammonium chloride (NH_4Cl) is heated

➤ Heating hydrated copper(II) sulfate:

Heat
$CuSO_4 \cdot 5H_2O_{(s)} \rightleftharpoons CuSO_{4(s)} + 5H_2O_{(g)}$
blue   white

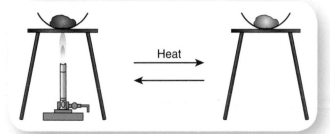

Heat

If the forward reaction is endothermic (absorbs heat) then the reverse reaction must be exothermic (releases heat).

Write out the column and row headings from the table in the 'changing temperature' section on page 59. Write out all of the four effects on separate pieces of paper and practise placing them in the right box.

HT

Equilibrium

When a reversible reaction is carried out in a closed system (nothing enters or leaves) and the rate of the forward reaction is equal to the rate of the reverse reaction, the reaction is said to have reached **equilibrium**.

HT Equilibrium conditions

The relative amounts of reactants and products at equilibrium depend on the **reaction conditions**. The effect of changing conditions on reactions at equilibrium can be predicted by Le Chatelier's principle, which states that 'for a reversible reaction, if changes are made to the concentration, temperature or pressure (for gaseous reactions) then the system responds to counteract the change'.

Changing concentration

If the concentration of one of the reactants is increased, more products will be formed (to use up the extra reactant) until equilibrium is established again (i.e. the equilibrium moves to the right until a new equilibrium is established). Similarly, if the concentration of one of the products is increased, more reactants will be formed (i.e. the equilibrium moves to the left until a new equilibrium is established).

Changing temperature

Forward reaction	Effect of increasing temperature	Effect of decreasing temperature
Endothermic	Equilibrium moves to right-hand side (i.e. forward reaction)	Equilibrium moves to left-hand side (i.e. reverse reaction)
Exothermic	Equilibrium moves to left-hand side	Equilibrium moves to right-hand side

Changing pressure

In order to predict the effect of changing pressure, the number of molecules of gas on each side of the equation needs to be known:

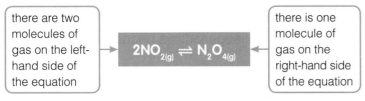

there are two molecules of gas on the left-hand side of the equation

$$2NO_{2(g)} \rightleftharpoons N_2O_{4(g)}$$

there is one molecule of gas on the right-hand side of the equation

If the pressure on a reaction at equilibrium is **increased**, the equilibrium shifts to the side of the equation with the **fewer** molecules of gas. In this case, increasing the pressure will shift the reaction to the right-hand side (i.e. producing more N_2O_4).

1. Which symbol is used to represent a reversible reaction?
2. The forward reaction in a reversible reaction is exothermic. Is the reverse reaction exothermic or endothermic?
HT 3. Consider the following reaction at equilibrium.

$$N_{2(g)} + 3H_{2(g)} \rightleftharpoons 2NH_{3(g)}$$

What is the effect on the amount of nitrogen at equilibrium of...
a) Increasing the concentration of hydrogen?
b) Increasing the pressure?

Mind map

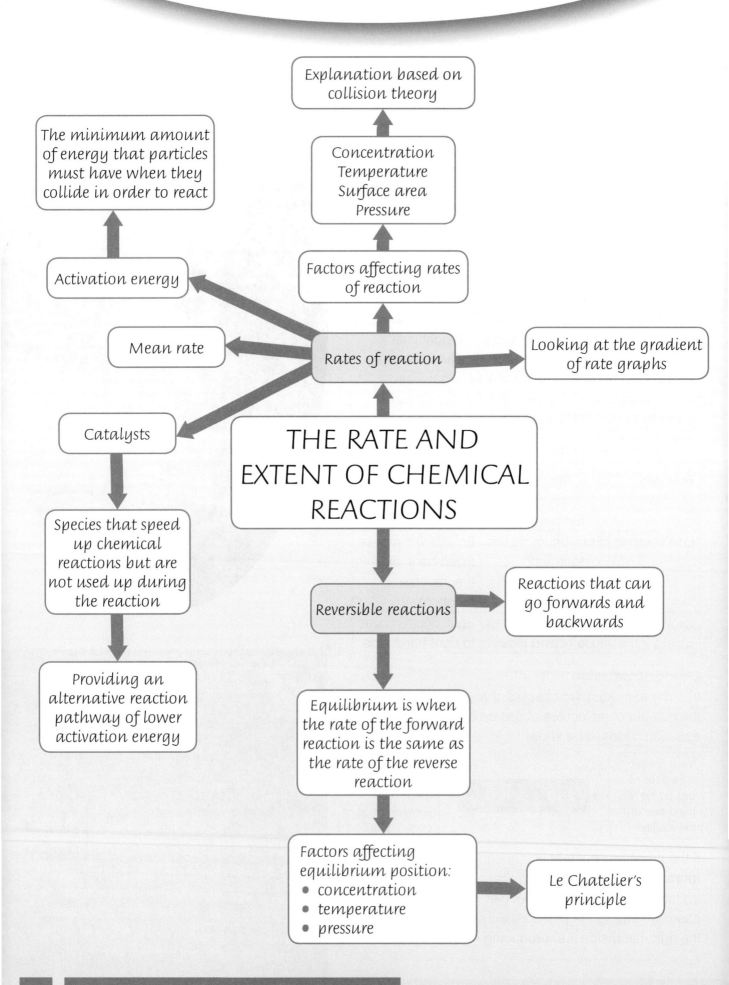

Explanation based on collision theory

The minimum amount of energy that particles must have when they collide in order to react

Concentration
Temperature
Surface area
Pressure

Activation energy

Factors affecting rates of reaction

Mean rate

Rates of reaction

Looking at the gradient of rate graphs

Catalysts

THE RATE AND EXTENT OF CHEMICAL REACTIONS

Species that speed up chemical reactions but are not used up during the reaction

Reversible reactions

Reactions that can go forwards and backwards

Providing an alternative reaction pathway of lower activation energy

Equilibrium is when the rate of the forward reaction is the same as the rate of the reverse reaction

Factors affecting equilibrium position:
- concentration
- temperature
- pressure

Le Chatelier's principle

Practice questions

1. A student was investigating the rate of reaction between magnesium and hydrochloric acid. He measured out a 0.25 g strip of magnesium metal and then added it to 25 cm³ of acid in a conical flask. A gas syringe was attached as shown in the diagram.

   The volume of hydrogen collected was recorded every 10 seconds. A graph of the student's results is shown below.

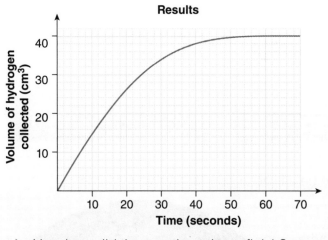

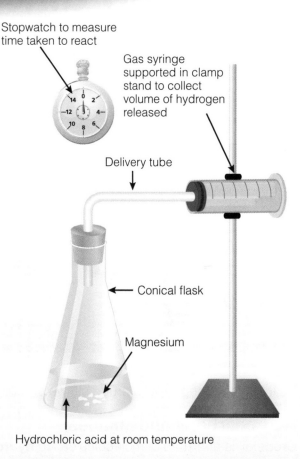

Stopwatch to measure time taken to react

Gas syringe supported in clamp stand to collect volume of hydrogen released

Delivery tube

Conical flask

Magnesium

Hydrochloric acid at room temperature

   a) How long did the reaction take to finish? Explain your answer. **(2 marks)**

   b) Using your answer to part **a**, calculate the mean rate of reaction. **(2 marks)**

   c) How can you tell from the graph that the rate of reaction was faster after 10 seconds than it was after 40 seconds? **(1 mark)**

   d) The student then repeated the experiment using 0.25 g of magnesium powder instead of magnesium ribbon. Everything else was kept the same. Sketch on the graph the curve that the results from this experiment would have produced. **(2 marks)**

   e) The student predicted that carrying out the experiment with a higher concentration of acid would have increased the rate of reaction. Explain why he is correct. **(2 marks)**

2. Hydrogen for use in the Haber process or in fuel cells can be produced from methane and water according to the equation below.

$$CH_{4(g)} + H_2O_{(g)} \rightleftharpoons CO_{(g)} + 3H_{2(g)}$$

   The forward reaction is endothermic.

   a) How can you tell that this process is carried out at a temperature above 100°C? **(1 mark)**

   b) What does the $\rightleftharpoons$ symbol tell you about the reaction? **(1 mark)**

   c) Explain why increasing the pressure on the equilibrium mixture will decrease the yield of hydrogen. **(1 mark)**

   d) State and explain the effect on the yield of hydrogen of increasing the temperature of the equilibrium mixture. **(2 marks)**

Crude oil, hydrocarbons and alkanes

Crude oil

This process describes how crude oil is formed.

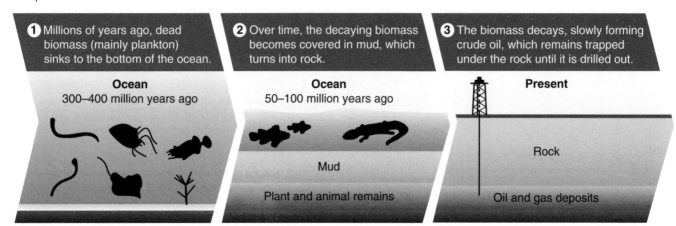

1 Millions of years ago, dead biomass (mainly plankton) sinks to the bottom of the ocean.

Ocean
300–400 million years ago

2 Over time, the decaying biomass becomes covered in mud, which turns into rock.

Ocean
50–100 million years ago

Mud

Plant and animal remains

3 The biomass decays, slowly forming crude oil, which remains trapped under the rock until it is drilled out.

Present

Rock

Oil and gas deposits

As it takes so long to form crude oil, we consider it to be a finite or non-renewable resource.

Hydrocarbons and alkanes

Crude oil is a mixture of molecules called **hydrocarbons**. Most hydrocarbons are members of a homologous series of molecules called alkanes.

Members of an homologous series…
➤ have the same general formula
➤ differ by CH_2 in their molecular formula from neighbouring compounds
➤ show a gradual trend in physical properties, e.g. boiling point
➤ have similar chemical properties.

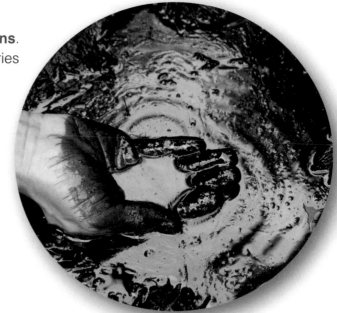

Alkanes are hydrocarbons that have the general formula C_nH_{2n+2}.

Alkane	Methane, CH_4	Ethane, C_2H_6	Propane, C_3H_8	Butane, C_4H_{10}
Displayed formula	H | H−C−H | H	H H | | H−C−C−H | | H H	H H H | | | H−C−C−C−H | | | H H H	H H H H | | | | H−C−C−C−C−H | | | | H H H H

Fractional distillation

Crude oil on its own is relatively useless. It is separated into more useful components (called fractions) by **fractional distillation**. The larger the molecule, the stronger the intermolecular forces and so the higher the boiling point.

Crude oil is heated until it evaporates.

It then enters a fractionating column which is hotter at the bottom than at the top

where the molecules condense at different temperatures.

Groups of molecules with similar boiling points are collected together. They are called fractions.

The fractions are sent for processing to produce fuels and feedstock (raw materials) for the petrochemical industry

which produces many useful materials, e.g. solvents, lubricants, detergents and polymers (plastics).

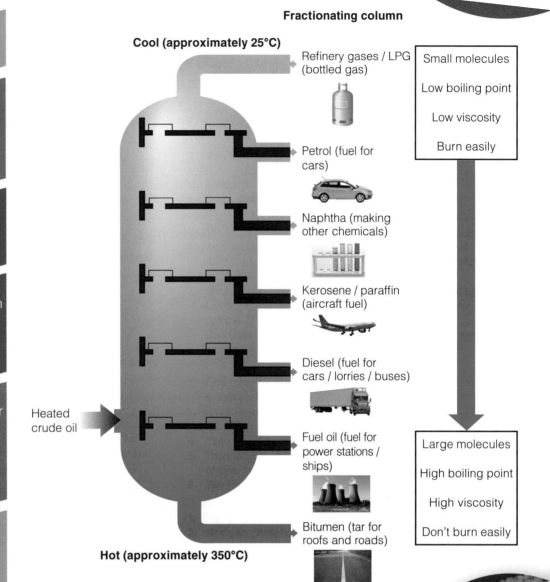

Fractionating column

Cool (approximately 25°C)

Refinery gases / LPG (bottled gas)

Petrol (fuel for cars)

Naphtha (making other chemicals)

Kerosene / paraffin (aircraft fuel)

Diesel (fuel for cars / lorries / buses)

Heated crude oil

Fuel oil (fuel for power stations / ships)

Bitumen (tar for roofs and roads)

Hot (approximately 350°C)

Small molecules

Low boiling point

Low viscosity

Burn easily

Large molecules

High boiling point

High viscosity

Don't burn easily

Combustion of hydrocarbons

Some of the fractions of crude oil (e.g. petrol and kerosene) are used as fuels. Burning these fuels releases energy. Combustion (burning) reactions are oxidation reactions. When the fuel is fully combusted, the carbon in the hydrocarbons is oxidised to carbon dioxide and the hydrogen is oxidised to water. For example, the combustion of methane:

$$CH_{4(g)} + 2O_{2(g)} \rightarrow CO_{2(g)} + 2H_2O_{(l)}$$

Cracking and alkenes

Cracking and alkenes

Many of the long-chain hydrocarbons found in crude oil are not very useful. **Cracking** is the process of turning a long-chain hydrocarbon into shorter, more useful ones.

Long-chain hydrocarbon

Short-chain hydrocarbons

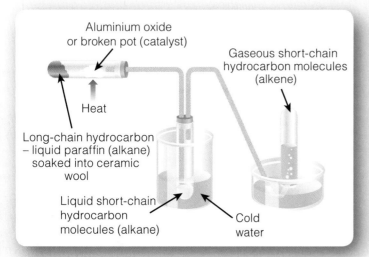

Cracking is done by passing hydrocarbon vapour over a hot catalyst or mixing the hydrocarbon vapour with steam before heating it to a very high temperature.

The diagram shows how cracking can be carried out in the laboratory.

Aluminium oxide or broken pot (catalyst)

Gaseous short-chain hydrocarbon molecules (alkene)

Heat

Long-chain hydrocarbon – liquid paraffin (alkane) soaked into ceramic wool

Liquid short-chain hydrocarbon molecules (alkane)

Cold water

Cracking produces alkanes and alkenes. The small-molecule alkanes that are formed during cracking are in high demand as fuels. The alkenes are mostly used to make plastics by the process of polymerisation.

There are many different equations that can represent cracking. This is because the long hydrocarbon can break in many different places. A typical equation for the cracking of the hydrocarbon decane ($C_{10}H_{22}$) is:

$$C_{10}H_{22} \rightarrow C_8H_{18} + C_2H_4$$

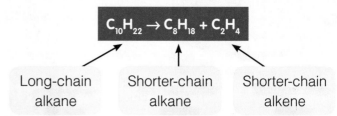

Long-chain alkane   Shorter-chain alkane   Shorter-chain alkene

The presence of alkenes can be detected using bromine water. Alkenes decolourise bromine water but when it is mixed with alkanes, the bromine water stays orange.

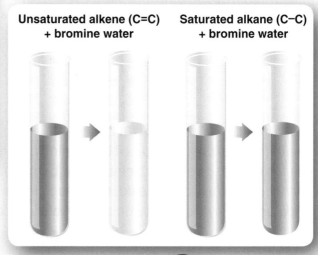

Unsaturated alkene (C=C) + bromine water   Saturated alkane (C–C) + bromine water

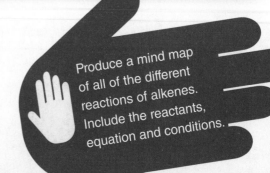

Produce a mind map of all of the different reactions of alkenes. Include the reactants, equation and conditions.

Alkenes

Alkenes are hydrocarbons with a carbon–carbon double bond. Molecules with carbon–carbon double bonds are called **unsaturated** molecules because there are two fewer hydrogen atoms than an alkane with the same number of carbon atoms. The general formula for the alkene homologous series is C_nH_{2n}.

Alkene	Ethene, C_2H_4	Propene, C_3H_6	Butene (but-1-ene), C_4H_8	But-2-ene, C_4H_8	Pent-1-ene, C_5H_{10}
Displayed Formula					

Alkenes usually **react** by atoms adding across the carbon–carbon double bond.

Reactant	Notes	Equation
Oxygen	Alkenes react with oxygen in combustion reactions. Incomplete combustion occurs when alkenes do not completely oxidise. When alkenes burn with a sooty flame incomplete combustion is taking place.	e.g. the complete combustion of ethene: $$C_2H_{4(g)} + 3O_2 \rightarrow 2CO_{2(g)} + 3H_2O_{(l)}$$
Hydrogen	Hydrogen atoms add across the carbon–carbon double bond so that a carbon–carbon single bond remains.	A nickel catalyst is required, e.g. when ethene reacts with hydrogen, ethane is formed:
Water	One of the hydrogen atoms in water adds to one side of the carbon–carbon double bond. The remaining OH atoms add to the other carbon atom.	This reaction takes place at a high temperature so that the water is present as steam. An acid catalyst (e.g. concentrated sulfuric acid) is required: e.g. ethene reacts with steam to form the alcohol ethanol.
Halogens (e.g. Cl_2 / Br_2)	Halogen atoms add across the carbon–carbon double bond so that a carbon–carbon single bond remains.	Ethene reacts with bromine to form dibromoethane:

Other alkenes react in the same way as ethene. This is because all alkenes contain the same **functional group**, for example, the reaction of propene with bromine:

Alcohols and carboxylic acids

Alcohols

Alcohols contain the functional group –OH. The first four members of the homologous series of alcohols are shown in the table.

Alcohol (all names end in 'ol')	Displayed formula	Structural formula (always ends in –OH)
Methanol	H | H—C—O—H | H	CH_3OH
Ethanol	H H | | H—C—C—O—H | | H H	CH_3CH_2OH
Propanol	H H H | | | H—C—C—C—O—H | | | H H H	$CH_3CH_2CH_2OH$
Butanol	H H H H | | | | H—C—C—C—C—O—H | | | | H H H H	$CH_3CH_2CH_2CH_2OH$

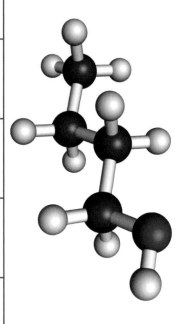

Alcohols…

➤ dissolve in water to form neutral solutions
➤ react with sodium to produce hydrogen
➤ burn in air to produce carbon dioxide and water

For example: $C_2H_5OH_{(l)} + 3O_{2(g)} \rightarrow 2CO_{2(g)} + 3H_2O_{(l)}$

➤ can be oxidised by acidified potassium manganate(VII) to form carboxylic acids.

Aqueous solutions of ethanol are produced by the anaerobic **fermentation** of sugar solution by yeast at 30ºC. The product can be distilled to produce a more concentrated solution of ethanol. Ethanol is the alcohol in alcoholic drinks.

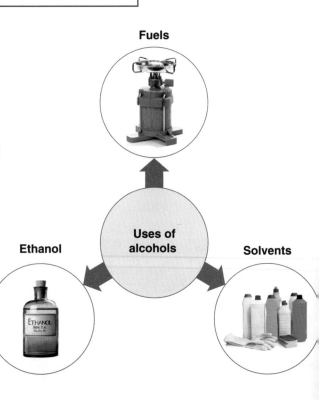

Fuels

Ethanol

Uses of alcohols

Solvents

Carboxylic acids

Carboxylic acids contain the functional group –COOH. The first four members of the homologous series of carboxylic acids are shown in the table.

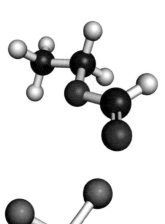

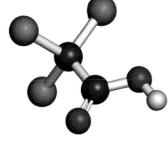

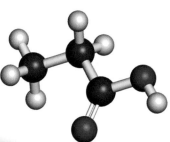

Alcohol (all names end in '…oic acid')	Displayed formula	Structural formula (always ends in COOH)
Methanoic acid	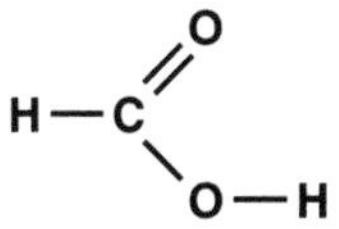	$HCOOH$
Ethanoic acid	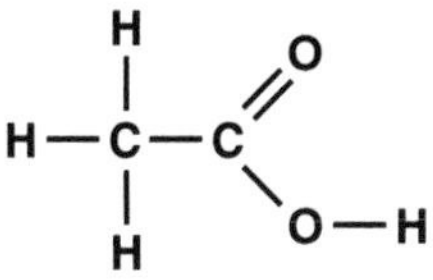	CH_3COOH
Propanoic acid	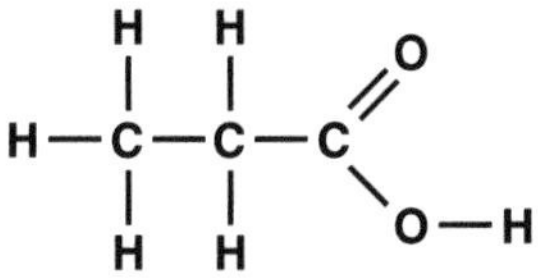	CH_3CH_2COOH
Butanoic acid	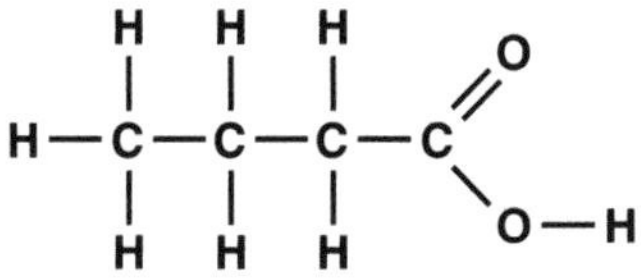	$CH_3CH_2CH_2COOH$

Carboxylic acids…

➤ Dissolve in water to form acidic solutions
➤ React with carbonates to form carbon dioxide
➤ Are weak acids, i.e. they do not completely ionise when dissolved in water
➤ React with alcohols in the presence of an acid catalyst to produce esters.

For example: ethanoic acid reacts with ethanol to produce water and the ester ethyl ethanoate.

Ethyl ethanoate

Citric acid and vitamin C

Malt vinegar

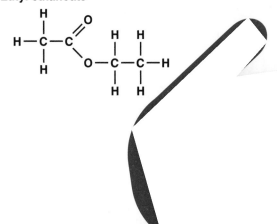

Polymerisation and natural polymers

Addition polymerisation

Addition polymerisation is the process of joining lots of small molecules (**monomers**) together to form very large molecules (**polymers**). The monomers must be alkenes because a carbon–carbon double bond is needed for addition polymerisation to occur.

Ethene monomers (unsaturated) → **Poly(ethene) polymers (saturated)**

$$\begin{array}{ccc} \overset{\displaystyle H\quad H}{\underset{\displaystyle H\quad H}{C=C}} + \overset{\displaystyle H\quad H}{\underset{\displaystyle H\quad H}{C=C}} + \longrightarrow & \overset{\displaystyle H\ H\ H\ H}{\underset{\displaystyle H\ H\ H\ H}{-C-C-C-C-}} \end{array}$$

...and thousands more...   ...and on and on...

The general equation below can be used to represent the formation of any addition polymer.

Poly(propene)

$$n\left[\begin{array}{c} H\ \ CH_3 \\ C=C \\ H\ \ H \end{array}\right] \longrightarrow \left[\begin{array}{c} H\ \ CH_3 \\ C-C \\ H\ \ H \end{array}\right]_n$$

The repeat unit in an addition polymer has the same atoms as the monomer because there are no other molecules formed in the reaction.

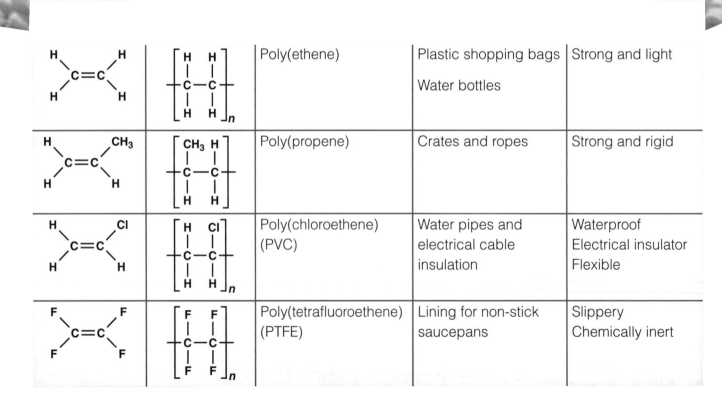

Monomer	Polymer	Name	Uses	Properties
$\overset{H}{\underset{H}{}}C=C\overset{H}{\underset{H}{}}$	$\left[\begin{array}{c}H\ H\\C-C\\H\ H\end{array}\right]_n$	Poly(ethene)	Plastic shopping bags Water bottles	Strong and light
$\overset{H}{\underset{H}{}}C=C\overset{CH_3}{\underset{H}{}}$	$\left[\begin{array}{c}CH_3\ H\\C-C\\H\ H\end{array}\right]$	Poly(propene)	Crates and ropes	Strong and rigid
$\overset{H}{\underset{H}{}}C=C\overset{Cl}{\underset{H}{}}$	$\left[\begin{array}{c}H\ Cl\\C-C\\H\ H\end{array}\right]_n$	Poly(chloroethene) (PVC)	Water pipes and electrical cable insulation	Waterproof Electrical insulator Flexible
$\overset{F}{\underset{F}{}}C=C\overset{F}{\underset{F}{}}$	$\left[\begin{array}{c}F\ F\\C-C\\F\ F\end{array}\right]_n$	Poly(tetrafluoroethene) (PTFE)	Lining for non-stick saucepans	Slippery Chemically inert

HT Condensation polymerisation

Condensation polymerisation takes place when the monomer has two functional groups in the molecule, such as ethane diol, which contains an alcohol (–OH) functional group at each end of the molecule.

$$HO-\underset{\underset{H}{|}}{\overset{\overset{H}{|}}{C}}-\underset{\underset{H}{|}}{\overset{\overset{H}{|}}{C}}-OH$$

Hexanedioic acid is a molecule that contains a carboxylic acid group (–COOH) at each end of the molecule.

$$\underset{HO}{\overset{O}{\diagdown}}C-(CH_2)_4-C\underset{OH}{\overset{O}{\diagup}}$$

Alcohols react with carboxylic acids to form esters (see Module 27). These two molecules polymerise to form a polyester. In condensation polymerisation, a small molecule (usually water) is also produced.

Ethane diol   Hexanedioic acid

↓

Repeat unit of polyester

In this diagram, blocks ☐ are used to represent the carbon chains in each monomer molecule (i.e. CH_2CH_2 and $CH_2CH_2CH_2CH_2$), as these are not involved in the polymerisation reaction.

Amino acids

Amino acids have two different functional groups in a molecule. Amino acid molecules react with each other to form polypeptides. Different amino acids can be combined in the same chain to form proteins.

Glycine is an amino acid with the formula H_2NCH_2COOH.

$$\underset{H}{\overset{H}{\diagdown}}N-\underset{\underset{H}{|}}{\overset{\overset{H}{|}}{C}}-C\underset{O-H}{\overset{O}{\diagup\diagup}}$$

Glycine undergoes condensation polymerisation (the NH_2 functional group in one molecule reacts with the –COOH functional group in another) to form the polypeptide $(-HNCH_2COO-)_n$

$$n\,H_2NCH_2COOH \rightarrow (-HNCH_2COO-)_n + nH_2O$$

DNA

DNA (deoxyribonucleic acid) is a large molecule that is essential for life. DNA encodes genetic instructions for the development and functioning of living organisms and viruses.

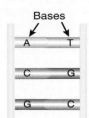

Most DNA molecules are two polymer chains, made from four different monomers called nucleotides. These are arranged in the form of a double helix.

DNA double helix

A section of the double helix

Other naturally occurring polymers

There are many polymers found in nature that are important for life. For example:

➤ proteins
➤ starch and cellulose

Starch and cellulose are polymers of sugars. Sugars, starch and cellulose are carbohydrates.

Protein-rich foods

Mind map

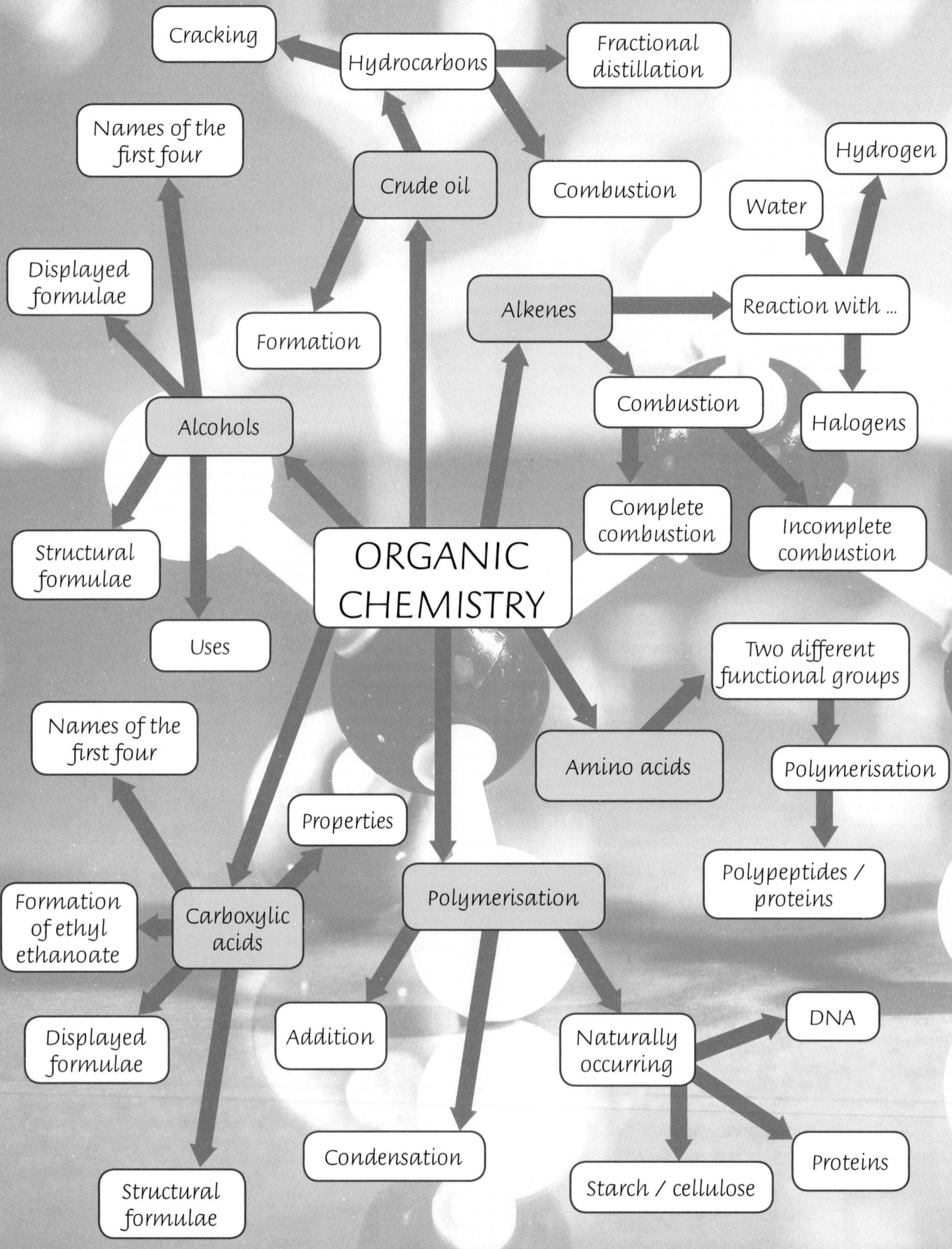

Cracking

Hydrocarbons

Fractional distillation

Names of the first four

Crude oil

Combustion

Hydrogen

Water

Displayed formulae

Alkenes

Reaction with ...

Formation

Combustion

Halogens

Alcohols

Structural formulae

Complete combustion

Incomplete combustion

ORGANIC CHEMISTRY

Uses

Two different functional groups

Names of the first four

Amino acids

Polymerisation

Properties

Polypeptides / proteins

Formation of ethyl ethanoate

Carboxylic acids

Polymerisation

DNA

Displayed formulae

Addition

Naturally occurring

Condensation

Starch / cellulose

Proteins

Structural formulae

Practice questions

1. Crude oil is extracted from the earth by drilling and then it is separated into useful components. Some of the alkanes found in crude oil undergo further processing to make them more useful in a process called cracking.

   a) Describe the stages in the formation of crude oil. **(3 marks)**

   b) What is the name of the process by which crude oil is separated and by what property are the molecules in crude oil separated? **(2 marks)**

   c) What are alkanes? **(2 marks)**

   d) Why is cracking an important process? **(2 marks)**

   e) State one way in which cracking can be carried out. **(1 mark)**

   f) The hydrocarbon dodecane ($C_{12}H_{26}$) can be cracked to produce two molecules of ethene (C_2H_4) and one other molecule. Complete the equation below stating the formula of this other product.

   $$C_{12}H_{26} \rightarrow 2C_2H_4 + \text{.............................}$$ **(1 mark)**

2. There are two main types of polymerisation. Poly(propene) is a polymer made from propene. Nylon is a polyester formed by condensation polymerisation.

   a) What method of polymerisation is used to form poly(propene)? **(1 mark)**

   b) What feature of a propene molecule means that it is able to undergo this type of polymerisation? **(1 mark)**

   c) Name a naturally occurring condensation polymer. **(1 mark)**

3. The alcohol ethanol can be made by reacting ethene with steam.

   a) Write a balanced symbol equation for this reaction. **(2 marks)**

   b) Suggest a suitable catalyst for this reaction. **(1 mark)**

   c) Name the gas produced when ethanol reacts with sodium. **(1 mark)**

   d) Draw the displayed formula of the carboxylic acid formed when ethanol is oxidised by potassium manganate(VII). **(1 mark)**

   e) Name the ester formed when ethanol reacts with ethanoic acid. **(1 mark)**

Purity, formulations and chromatography

Purity

In everyday language, a pure substance can mean a substance that has had nothing added to it (i.e. in its natural state), such as milk.

In chemistry, a pure substance is a single element or compound (i.e. not mixed with any other substance).

Pure elements and compounds melt and boil at specific temperatures. For example, pure water freezes at 0°C and boils at 100°C. However, if something is added to water (e.g. salt) then the freezing point decreases (i.e. goes below 0°C) and the boiling point rises above 100°C.

Formulations

A **formulation** is a mixture that has been designed as a useful product. Many formulations are complex mixtures in which each ingredient has a specific purpose.

Formulations are made by mixing the individual components in carefully measured quantities to ensure that the product has the correct properties.

Fuels

Cleaning materials

Fertilisers

Examples of formulations

Paints

Foods

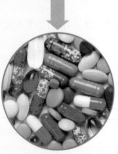
Medicines

Find five items at home or in a supermarket that are described as 'pure'. Look at their composition (e.g. from a food label) and decide whether they are chemically pure.

Chromatography

Chromatography is used to separate mixtures of dyes. It is used to help identify substances.

In paper chromatography, a solvent (the mobile phase) moves up the paper (the stationary phase) carrying different components of the mixture different distances, depending on their attraction for the paper and the solvent. In thin layer chromatography (TLC), the stationary phase is a thin layer of an inert substance (e.g. silica) supported on a flat, unreactive surface (e.g. a glass plate).

In the chromatogram on the right, substance X is being analysed and compared with samples A, B, C, D and E.

It can be seen from the chromatogram that substance X has the same pattern of spots as sample D. This means that sample X and sample D are the same substance. Pure compounds (e.g. compound A) will only produce one spot on a chromatogram.

The ratio of the distance moved by the compound to the distance moved by the solvent is known as its R_f value.

$$R_f = \frac{\text{distance moved by substance}}{\text{distance moved by solvent}}$$

Different compounds have different R_f values in different solvents. This can be used to help identify unknown compounds by comparing R_f values with known substances.

In this case, the R_f value is 0.73 $\left(\frac{4.0}{5.5}\right)$ ⟶

In **gas chromatography** (GC), the mobile phase is an inert gas (e.g. helium). The stationary phase is a very thin layer of an inert liquid on a solid support, such as beads of silica packed into a long thin tube. GC is a more sensitive method than TLC for separating mixtures, and it allows you to determine the amount of each chemical in the mixture.

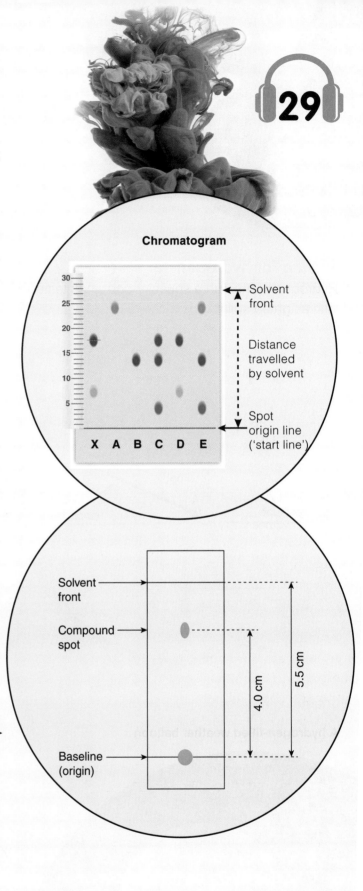

Identification of gases

Testing for hydrogen

Hydrogen burns with a squeaky *pop* when tested with a lighted splint.

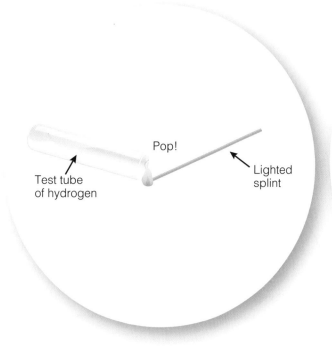

Pop!

Test tube of hydrogen

Lighted splint

Testing for oxygen

Oxygen relights a glowing splint.

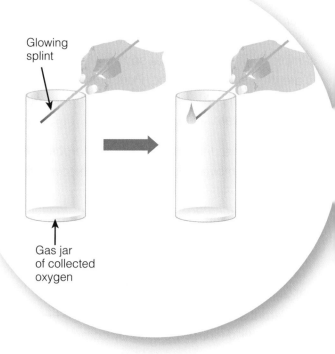

Glowing splint

Gas jar of collected oxygen

A hydrogen-filled weather balloon

Oxygen is used in breathing masks

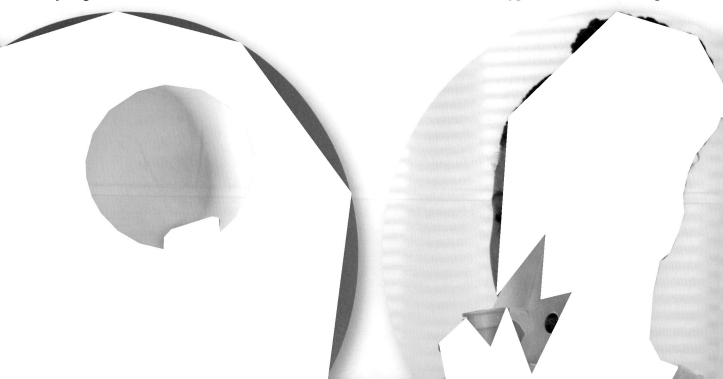

Carbon dioxide is releas[ed]
when fossil fuels are bu[rnt]

Testing for carbon dioxide

When carbon dioxide is mixed with or bubbled through limewater (calcium hydroxide solution) the limewater turns milky (cloudy).

Testing for chlorine

Chlorine turns moist blue litmus paper red before bleaching it and turning it white.

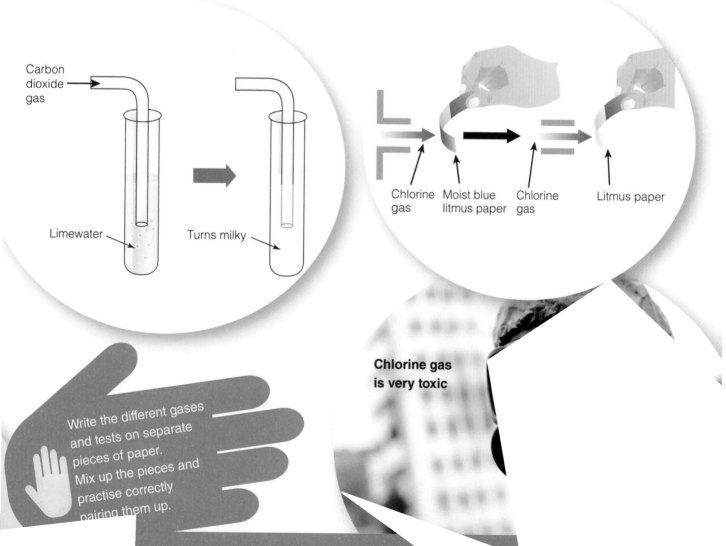

Carbon dioxide gas

Limewater — Turns milky

Chlorine gas — Moist blue litmus paper — Chlorine gas — Litmus paper

Chlorine gas is very toxic

Write the different gases and tests on separate pieces of paper. Mix up the pieces and practise correctly pairing them up.

Which gas relights a glowing splint?
What is the test for hydrogen gas?
What is the chemical name for limewater?
What happens to limewater when it is mixed with carbon dioxide ga[s]?
What effect does chlorine gas have on moist blue litmus paper?

31

Identification of cations

Flame tests

Flame tests can be used to identify metal **ions**.

Lithium, sodium, potassium, calcium and copper compounds can be recognised by the distinctive colours they produce in a flame test.

To do a flame test, follow this method:

1 Heat and then dip a piece of nichrome (a nickel–chromium alloy) wire in concentrated hydrochloric acid to clean it.

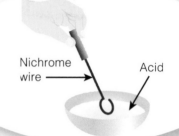

Nichrome wire →   Acid

2 Dip the wire in the compound.

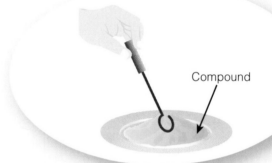

Compound

3 Put it into a Bunsen flame. Different colours will indicate the presence of certain ions.

The distinctive colours are:
➤ orange-red / brick red for **calcium** (Ca^{2+})
➤ crimson red for **lithium** (Li^+)
➤ lilac for **potassium** (K^+)
➤ yellow for **sodium** (Na^+)
➤ blue / green for **copper** (Cu^{2+}).

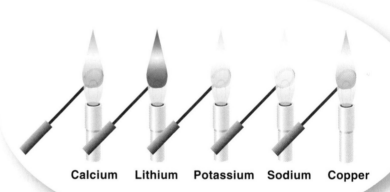

Calcium   **Lithium**   **Potassium**   **Sodium**   **Copper**

If a sample containing a mixture of ions is used then some flame colours can be masked.

Keyword

Precipitate ➤ A solid formed when two solutions react together

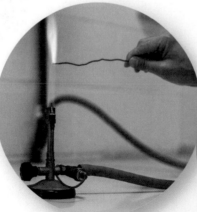

On separate cards, write the name or formula of the ions in this section. On other cards, write all the different colours of the flame tests or hydroxide precipitates – one on each card. Mix up the cards and try to pair them together.

Using sodium hydroxide

Metal compounds in solution contain **metal ions**. Some of these form **precipitates** – **insoluble** solids that come out of solution when sodium hydroxide solution is added to them.

For example, when sodium hydroxide solution is added to calcium chloride solution, a white precipitate of calcium hydroxide is formed (as well as sodium chloride solution). You can see how this precipitate is formed by considering the ions involved.

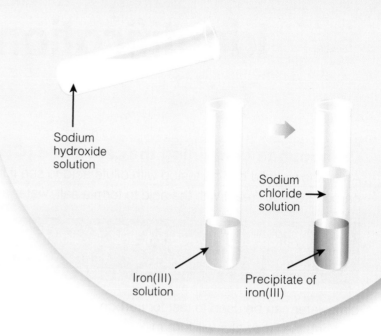

Sodium hydroxide solution

Sodium chloride solution

Iron(III) solution

Precipitate of iron(III)

The precipitates formed when metal ions are mixed with sodium hydroxide solution			
Metal ion	Precipitate formed		
	Precipitate	Precipitate colour	Equation for formation of precipitate
Aluminium $Al^{3+}_{(aq)}$	Aluminium hydroxide	White (dissolves with excess sodium hydroxide)	$Al^{3+}_{(aq)} + 3OH^-_{(aq)} \rightarrow Al(OH)_{3(s)}$
Calcium $Ca^{2+}_{(aq)}$	Calcium hydroxide	White	$Ca^{2+}_{(aq)} + 2OH^-_{(aq)} \rightarrow Ca(OH)_{2(s)}$
Magnesium $Mg^{2+}_{(aq)}$	Magnesium hydroxide	White	$Mg^{2+}_{(aq)} + 2OH^-_{(aq)} \rightarrow Mg(OH)_{2(s)}$
Copper(II) $Cu^{2+}_{(aq)}$	Copper(II) hydroxide	Blue	$Cu^{2+}_{(aq)} + 2OH^-_{(aq)} \rightarrow Cu(OH)_{2(s)}$
Iron(II) $Fe^{2+}_{(aq)}$	Iron(II) hydroxide	Green	$Fe^{2+}_{(aq)} + 2OH^-_{(aq)} \rightarrow Fe(OH)_{2(s)}$
Iron(III) $Fe^{3+}_{(aq)}$	Iron(III) hydroxide	Brown	$Fe^{3+}_{(aq)} + 3OH^-_{(aq)} \rightarrow Fe(OH)_{3(s)}$

1. Which metal gives a lilac flame in a flame test?
2. What colour flame is seen when a flame test is done on a compound containing lithium?
3. What is the name of the precipitate formed when a solution containing magnesium ions reacts with sodium hydroxide solution?
4. Write an equation for the formation of the precipitate formed when a solution containing Fe^{2+} ions reacts with sodium hydroxide.
5. What is the colour of the precipitate formed in question 4?

Identification of anions

Compounds containing the carbonate (CO_3^{2-}) ion

An unknown solid can be tested with dilute acid to see if it contains carbonate ions, CO_3^{2-}. If the solid is a carbonate, it will react with the acid to form a salt, water and carbon dioxide gas, which fizzes. For example:

> calcium carbonate + hydrochloric acid → calcium chloride + carbon dioxide + water
> $$CaCO_{3(s)} \quad + \quad 2HCl_{(aq)} \quad → \quad CaCl_{2(aq)} \quad + \quad CO_{2(g)} \quad + H_2O_{(l)}$$

Limewater can be used to test for carbon dioxide. If the gas is present, the limewater will turn milky / cloudy.

Most carbonate compounds are insoluble but some (e.g. sodium carbonate and potassium carbonate) are soluble in water and produce solutions containing carbonate ions.

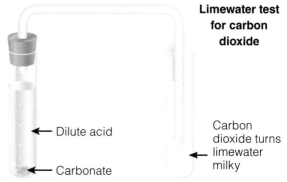

Limewater test for carbon dioxide

← Dilute acid

← Carbonate

Carbon dioxide turns limewater milky

Identifying dissolved ions

The **dissolved ions** of some salts are easy to identify as they will undergo **precipitation** reactions.

Sulfates (SO_4^{2-}) can be detected using dilute hydrochloric acid and barium chloride solution. A white precipitate of barium sulfate forms, as in the following example.

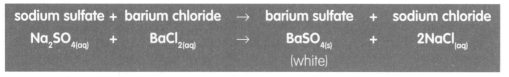

> sodium sulfate + barium chloride → barium sulfate + sodium chloride
> $$Na_2SO_{4(aq)} \quad + \quad BaCl_{2(aq)} \quad → \quad BaSO_{4(s)} \quad + \quad 2NaCl_{(aq)}$$
> (white)

32

Silver nitrate solution, in the presence of dilute nitric acid, is used to detect halide ions. Halides are the ions made by the halogens (group 7).

With silver nitrate:
➤ chlorides (Cl^-) form a white precipitate
➤ bromides (Br^-) form a cream precipitate
➤ iodides (I^-) form a pale yellow precipitate.

> sodium chloride + silver nitrate → silver chloride + sodium nitrate
> $$NaCl_{(aq)} \quad + \quad AgNO_{3(aq)} \quad → \quad AgCl_{(s)} \quad + \quad NaNO_{3(aq)}$$
> (white)

> sodium bromide + silver nitrate → silver bromide + sodium nitrate
> $$NaBr_{(aq)} \quad + \quad AgNO_{3(aq)} \quad → \quad AgBr_{(s)} \quad + \quad NaNO_{3(aq)}$$
> (cream)

> sodium bromide + silver nitrate → silver iodide + sodium nitrate
> $$NaI_{(aq)} \quad + \quad AgNO_{3(aq)} \quad → \quad AgI_{(s)} \quad + \quad NaNO_{3(aq)}$$
> (pale yellow)

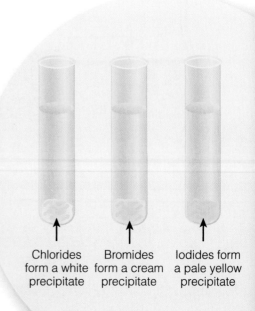

Chlorides form a white precipitate | Bromides form a cream precipitate | Iodides form a pale yellow precipitate

Instrumental methods of analysis

As well as chemical tests, elements and compounds can also be analysed and identified by instrumental methods.

Advantages of instrumental methods compared with chemical tests		
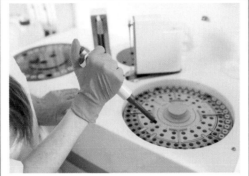		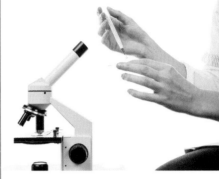
➤ More accurate	➤ More sensitive	➤ Can be used with very small samples

Flame emission spectroscopy

Flame emission spectroscopy can be used to identify metal ions present in solutions.

1. The sample is put into a flame.

2. The light given out is passed through a **spectroscope/flame photometer**.

3. A line spectrum is produced.

4. This is compared with reference spectra.

5. Metal ions present are identified.

6. The concentration of ions in solution can be determined by reference to a calibration curve.

The line spectra of some metals

The top scale shows the different wavelengths (λ) of light

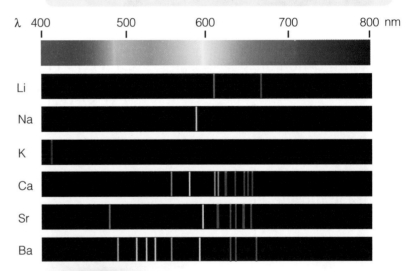

Make a table of all of the different anions on these pages and their tests and results.
Cover up the tests and results and see how many you can remember!

Keywords
Spectroscope/flame photometer ➤ A device for observing the spectrum of produced by

1. Which ion reacts with
2. What colour precipita ed when bromide ions rea
3. Name the solution us for the sulfate (SO_4^{2-}) ion after dilute hydrochloric acid has been added.
4. Give one advantage o an instrumental method of analysis over a chemica test.

Mind map

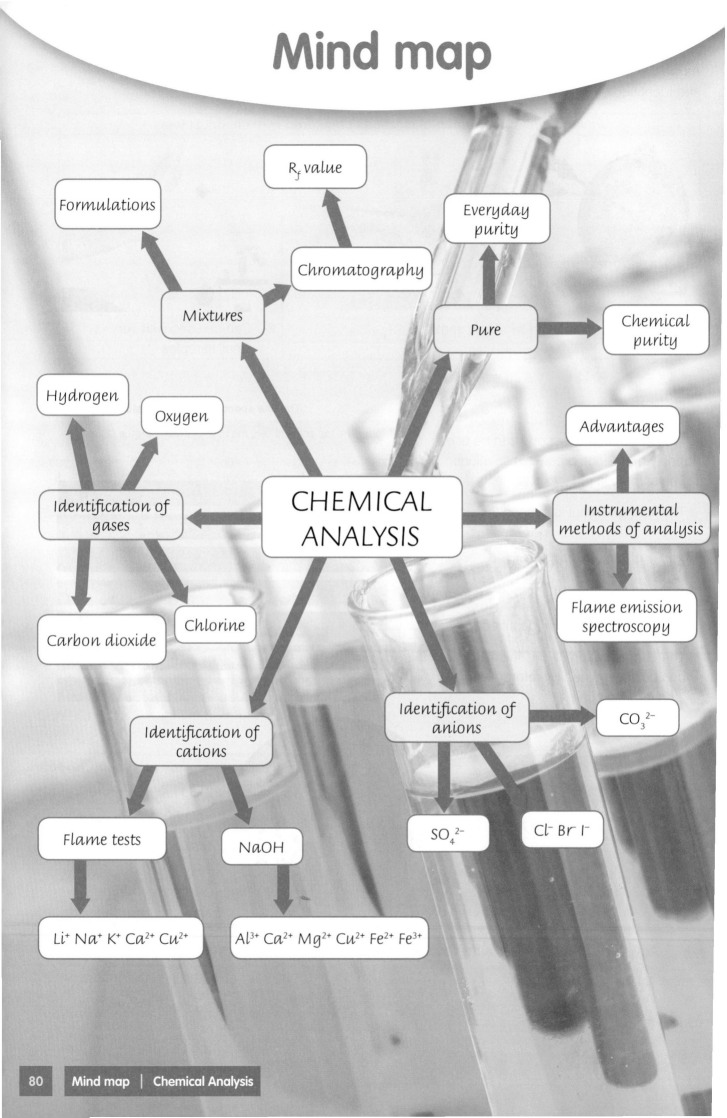

Formulations

R_f value

Everyday purity

Chromatography

Mixtures

Pure

Chemical purity

Hydrogen

Oxygen

Advantages

Identification of gases

CHEMICAL ANALYSIS

Instrumental methods of analysis

Flame emission spectroscopy

Carbon dioxide

Chlorine

Identification of cations

Identification of anions

CO_3^{2-}

Flame tests

NaOH

SO_4^{2-}

Cl^- Br^- I^-

Li^+ Na^+ K^+ Ca^{2+} Cu^{2+}

Al^{3+} Ca^{2+} Mg^{2+} Cu^{2+} Fe^{2+} Fe^{3+}

Practice questions

1. Potassium sulfate is a white solid commonly used in fertilisers.

   It contains potassium ions (K^+) and sulfate ions (SO_4^{2-}).

   A flame test can be carried out to confirm the presence of potassium in solid potassium sulfate.

   a) State the formula of potassium sulfate. **(1 mark)**

   b) Describe how to carry out a flame test. **(3 marks)**

   c) What colour flame would be observed when a flame test is carried out using potassium sulfate? **(1 mark)**

   To confirm the presence of the sulfate ion, the solid needs to be dissolved in water before adding two chemicals.

   d) Name the two chemicals that need to be added to this solution in order to test for the presence of the sulfate ion. **(2 marks)**

   e) What would be observed if the sulfate ion is present? **(2 marks)**

   f) Name an instrumental method that can be used to determine the presence of potassium ions in a sample of fertiliser. **(1 mark)**

2. Compound X produced a red flame in a flame test.
   When dilute hydrochloric acid was added to compound X, a gas was produced that turned limewater milky.

   a) Give the formula of the cation present in compound X. **(1 mark)**

   b) Name the gas produced when dilute hydrochloric acid was added to X. **(1 mark)**

   c) Give the formula of the anion present in compound X. **(1 mark)**

   d) What is the formula of compound X? **(1 mark)**

   e) Describe how you would show that dilute hydrochloric acid contains the chloride ion. **(3 marks)**

Evolution of the atmosphere

The Earth's early atmosphere

Theories about the composition of Earth's early atmosphere and how the atmosphere was formed have changed over time. Evidence for the early atmosphere is limited because the Earth is approximately 4.6 billion years old.

The table below gives one theory to explain the evolution of the atmosphere.

Time scale	Condition of the atmosphere	Key factors and events that shaped the atmosphere

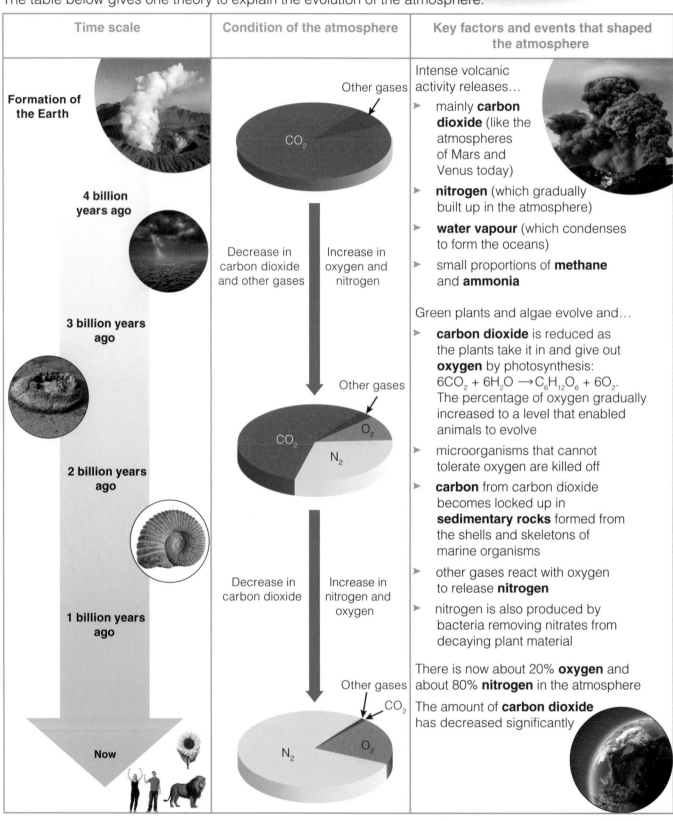

Formation of the Earth

4 billion years ago

Other gases

CO_2

Decrease in carbon dioxide and other gases — Increase in oxygen and nitrogen

Intense volcanic activity releases…
- mainly **carbon dioxide** (like the atmospheres of Mars and Venus today)
- **nitrogen** (which gradually built up in the atmosphere)
- **water vapour** (which condenses to form the oceans)
- small proportions of **methane** and **ammonia**

3 billion years ago

Other gases

CO_2 O_2 N_2

Decrease in carbon dioxide — Increase in nitrogen and oxygen

Green plants and algae evolve and…
- **carbon dioxide** is reduced as the plants take it in and give out **oxygen** by photosynthesis: $6CO_2 + 6H_2O \rightarrow C_6H_{12}O_6 + 6O_2$. The percentage of oxygen gradually increased to a level that enabled animals to evolve
- microorganisms that cannot tolerate oxygen are killed off
- **carbon** from carbon dioxide becomes locked up in **sedimentary rocks** formed from the shells and skeletons of marine organisms
- other gases react with oxygen to release **nitrogen**
- nitrogen is also produced by bacteria removing nitrates from decaying plant material

2 billion years ago

1 billion years ago

Now

Other gases CO_2

N_2 O_2

There is now about 20% **oxygen** and about 80% **nitrogen** in the atmosphere

The amount of **carbon dioxide** has decreased significantly

Composition of the atmosphere today

The proportions of gases in the atmosphere have been more or less the same for about 200 million years. **Water vapour** may also be present in varying quantities (0–3%).

Mainly argon, plus other noble gases (1%)

Carbon dioxide, CO_2 (0.03%)

Oxygen, O_2 (21%)

Nitrogen, N_2 (78%)

How carbon dioxide decreased

The amount of carbon dioxide in the atmosphere today is much less than it was when the atmosphere first formed. This is because…

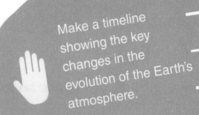

Make a timeline showing the key changes in the evolution of the Earth's atmosphere.

➤ green plants and algae use carbon dioxide for **photosynthesis**

➤ fossil fuels such as oil (see Module 25) and coal (a sedimentary rock made from thick plant deposits that were buried and compressed over millions of years) have captured CO_2.

➤ carbon dioxide is used to form sedimentary rocks, e.g. limestone

1. Name two gases that volcanoes released into the early atmosphere.
2. How did oxygen become present in the atmosphere?
3. How much of the atmosphere today is nitrogen gas?
4. State two ways that the amount of carbon dioxide present in the early atmosphere decreased.

Climate change

ⓦ Human activity and global warming

Some human activities increase the amounts of greenhouse gases in the atmosphere including...

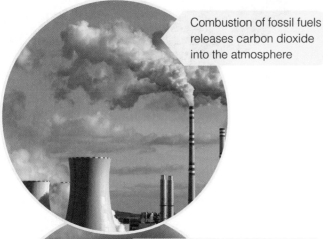

Combustion of fossil fuels releases carbon dioxide into the atmosphere

Increased animal farming releases more methane into the atmosphere, e.g. as a by-product of digestion and decomposition of waste

Deforestation reduces the amount of carbon dioxide removed from the atmosphere by photosynthesis

Decomposition of rubbish in landfill sites also releases methane into the atmosphere

Greenhouse gases

The temperature on Earth is maintained at a level to support life by the greenhouse gases in the atmosphere. These gases allow short wavelength radiation from the Sun to pass through but absorb the long wavelength radiation reflected back from the ground trapping heat and causing an increase in temperature. Common greenhouse gases are water vapour, carbon dioxide and methane.

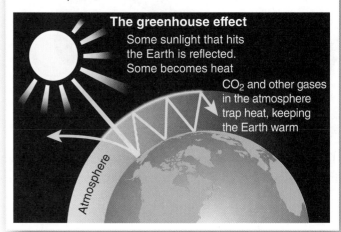

The greenhouse effect
Some sunlight that hits the Earth is reflected. Some becomes heat

CO_2 and other gases in the atmosphere trap heat, keeping the Earth warm

Atmosphere

The increase in carbon dioxide levels in the last century or so correlates with the increased use of fossil fuels by humans.

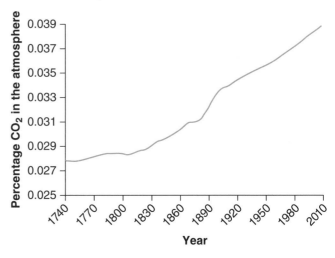

Based on **peer-reviewed evidence**, many scientists believe that increasing these human activities will lead to global climate change.

Predicting the impact of changes on global climate change is not easy because of the many different contributing factors involved. This can lead to simplified models and speculation often presented in the media that may not be based on all of the evidence. This means that the information could be biased.

Increased human activity resulting in more release of fossil fuels

Increased temperatures

Global climate change

Global climate change

Increasing average global temperature is a major cause of climate change. Potential effects of climate change include:

Rising sea levels, which may cause flooding and coastal erosion

More frequent and severe storms

Changes to the amount, timing and distribution of rainfall

Temperature and water stress for humans and wildlife

Changes in the food producing capacity of some regions

Changes to the distribution of wildlife species

Reducing the carbon footprint

The **carbon footprint** is a measure of the total amount of carbon dioxide (and other greenhouse gases) emitted over the life cycle of a product, service or event.

Problems of trying to reduce the carbon footprint include…

➤ disagreement over the causes and consequences of global climate change
➤ lack of public information and education
➤ lifestyle changes, e.g. greater use of cars / aeroplanes
➤ economic considerations, i.e. the financial costs of reducing the carbon footprint
➤ incomplete international co-operation.

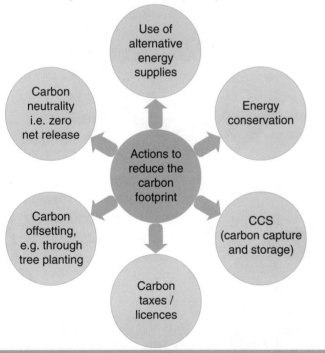

Use of alternative energy supplies

Carbon neutrality i.e. zero net release

Energy conservation

Actions to reduce the carbon footprint

Carbon offsetting, e.g. through tree planting

CCS (carbon capture and storage)

Carbon taxes / licences

Produce a leaflet informing members of the public about how they can reduce their own carbon footprint.

Keywords

Peer-reviewed evidence ➤ Work (evidence) of scientists that has been checked by other scientists to ensure that it is accurate and scientifically valid
Carbon footprint ➤ The total amount of carbon dioxide (and other greenhouse gases) emitted over the full life cycle of a product, service or event

1. Name two greenhouse gases.
2. State one way that human activity leads to an increased amount of methane in the atmosphere.
3. Give two potential effects of global climate change.
4. Give an example of one problem of trying to reduce the carbon footprint.

Atmospheric pollution

Pollutants from fuels

The combustion of **fossil fuels** is a major source of atmospheric pollutants. Most fuels contain carbon and often sulfur is present as an impurity. Many different gases are released into the atmosphere when a fuel is burned.

Solid particles and unburned hydrocarbons can also be released forming **particulates** in the air.

carbon monoxide

carbon dioxide

Gases produced by burning fuels

oxides of nitrogen

water vapour

sulfur dioxide

Sulfur dioxide is produced by the oxidation of sulfur present in fuels – often from coal-burning power stations

Carbon monoxide and soot (carbon) are produced by incomplete combustion of fuels

Oxides of nitrogen are formed from the reaction between nitrogen and oxygen from the air – often from the high temperatures and sparks in the engines of motor vehicles

Keywords

Fossil fuel ➤ Fuel formed in the ground over millions of years from the remains of dead plants and animal

Particulates ➤ Small solid particles present in the air

Properties and effects of atmospheric pollutants

Carbon monoxide is a colourless, odourless toxic gas and so it is difficult to detect. It combines with haemoglobin in the blood, which reduces the oxygen-carrying capacity of blood.

Sulfur dioxide and **oxides of nitrogen** cause respiratory problems in humans and can form acid rain in the atmosphere. Acid rain damages plants and buildings.

Particulates in the atmosphere can cause global dimming, which reduces the amount of sunlight that reaches the Earth's surface. Breathing in particulates can also damage lungs, which can cause health problems.

Make a list of all of the ways in one day that you see waste gases being released into the atmosphere.

1. Name two gases produced by burning fuels.
2. How is carbon monoxide formed?
3. What problems do atmospheric sulfur dioxide and oxides of nitrogen cause?

Using the Earth's resources and obtaining potable water

Earth's resources

We use the Earth's **resources** to provide us with warmth, shelter, food and transport. These needs are met from natural resources which, supplemented by agriculture, provide food, timber, clothing and fuels. Resources from the earth, atmosphere and oceans are processed to provide energy and materials.

Keywords

Sustainable development ➤ Living in a way that meets the needs of the current generation without compromising the potential of future generations to meet their own needs

Potable water ➤ Water that is safe to drink

Industrial chemical processes can be used to make new materials, reducing the demand for natural resources

Chemistry plays a role in providing sustainable development. This means that the needs of the current generation are met without compromising the potential of future generations to meet their own needs. For example…

Chemistry plays an important role in improving agricultural processes, e.g. by developing fertilisers

Drinking water

Water that is safe to drink is called potable water. It is not pure in the chemical sense (see Module 29) because it contains dissolved minerals and ions.

Water of appropriate quality is essential for life. This means that it contains sufficiently low levels of dissolved salts and microbes.

In the UK, most potable water comes from rainwater. To turn rainwater into potable water, water companies carry out a number of processes.

① An appropriate source of fresh water is selected

② It is then passed through filter beds to remove any solid impurities

③ Finally it is sterilised (suitable sterilising agents include chlorine, ozone and ultraviolet light) to kill microbes, making it safe to drink

Waste water

Urban lifestyles and industrial processes generate large quantities of waste water, which requires treatment before being released into the environment. Sewage and agricultural waste water require removal of organic matter and harmful microbes. Industrial waste water may require removal of organic matter and harmful chemicals.

Sewage treatment includes...
➤ screening and grit removal
➤ sedimentation to produce sewage sludge and effluent
➤ anaerobic digestion of sewage sludge
➤ aerobic biological treatment of effluent.

When supplies of fresh water are limited, removal of salt (desalination) of salty water / seawater can be used.

This is done in two ways:

➤ By distillation.

Thermometer →
Water out
Condenser
Distilling flask →
Salty water →
Water in
Receiving flask
Burner
Desalinated water

➤ By processes that use membranes, such as reverse osmosis.

External pressure
Fresh water
Seawater

However, these processes require large amounts of energy.

Find out different ways of making water potable.

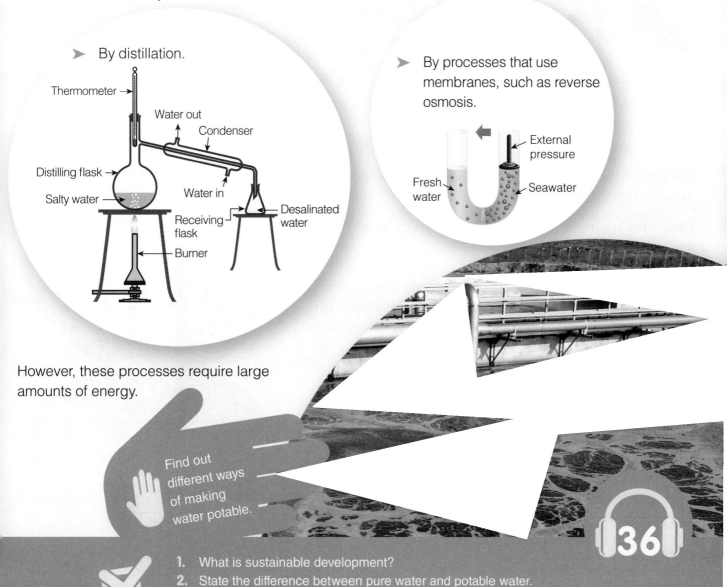

1. What is sustainable development?
2. State the difference between pure water and potable water.
3. What are the two main stages in turning rainwater into potable water?
4. Name one way of desalinating salty water.

Alternative methods of extracting metals

HT

Extracting copper

Copper is an important metal with lots of uses. It is used in electrical wiring because it is an excellent conductor of electricity. It is also used in water pipes because it conducts heat and does not corrode or react with the water.

The Earth's resources of metal **ores** are limited and copper ores are becoming scarce.

New ways of extracting copper from **low-grade ores** include…

➤ **phytomining**

  Phytomining uses plants to absorb metal compounds. This means that the plants accumulate metal within them. Harvesting and then burning the plants leaves ash that is rich in the metal compounds.

➤ **bioleaching**

  Bioleaching uses bacteria to extract metals from low-grade ores. A solution containing bacteria is mixed with a low-grade ore. The bacteria release the metals into solution (known as a leachate) where they can be easily extracted.

These new extraction methods reduce the impact on the Earth of mining, moving and disposing of large amounts of rock.

Processing metal compounds

The metal compounds from phytomining and bioleaching are processed to obtain the metal. Copper can be obtained from solutions of copper compounds by...

➤ **displacement** using scrap iron – iron is more reactive than copper, so placing iron into a solution of copper will result in copper metal being displaced.

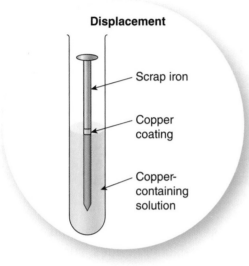

Displacement

- Scrap iron
- Copper coating
- Copper-containing solution

➤ **electrolysis**.

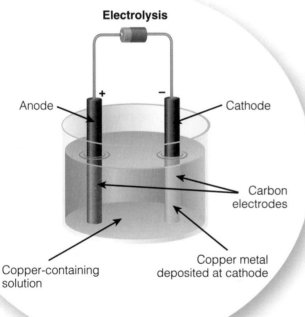

Electrolysis

- Anode +
- Cathode −
- Carbon electrodes
- Copper-containing solution
- Copper metal deposited at cathode

Keywords

Ore ➤ A naturally occurring mineral from which it is economically viable to extract a metal

Low-grade ores ➤ Ores that contain small amounts of metal

Phytomining ➤ A method of metal extraction that involves growing plants in metal solutions so that they accumulate metal; the plants are then burnt and the metal extracted from the ash

Bioleaching ➤ An extraction method that uses bacteria to extract metals from low-grade ores

Find examples of copper being used in your home. Think what properties of copper make it suitable for that use.

🎧 **37**

1. State one use of copper.
2. Why is it important to develop new ways of extracting metals?
3. Which biological method of extracting metals involves bacteria?
4. Give one way that metal can be extracted from a metal containing solution.

38

Life-cycle assessment and recycling

Life-cycle assessments

Life-cycle assessments (LCAs) are carried out to evaluate the environmental impact of products in each of the following stages.

| Extracting and processing raw materials | Manufacturing and packaging | Disposal at the end of useful life | Transport and distribution at each of the previous stages |

The following steps are considered when carrying out an LCA.

- How much energy is needed?
- How much water is used?
- What resources are required?
- How much waste is produced?
- How much pollution is produced?

Life-cycle assessment

Many of these values are relatively easy to quantify. However, some values, such as the amount of pollution, are often difficult to measure and so value judgements have to be made. This means that carrying out an LCA is not a purely objective process.

It is not always easy to obtain accurate figures. This means that selective or abbreviated LCAs, which are open to bias or misuse, can be devised to evaluate a product, to reinforce predetermined conclusions or to support claims for advertising purposes.

For example, look at the LCA below.

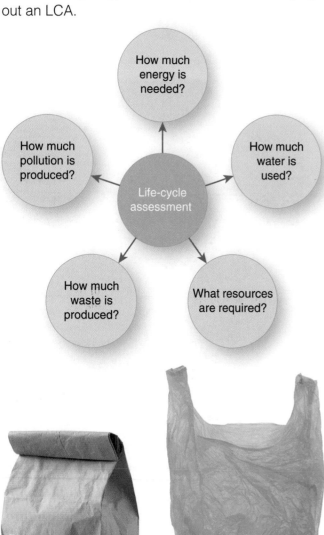

Example of an LCA for the use of plastic (polythene) and paper shopping bags		
	Amount per 1000 bags over the whole LCA	
	Paper	Plastic (polythene)
Energy use (MJ)	2590	713
Fossil fuel use (Kg)	28	13
Solid waste (Kg)	34	6
Greenhouse gas emissions (kg CO_2)	72	36
Freshwater use (litres)	3387	198

This LCA provides evidence supporting the argument that using polythene bags is better for the environment than paper bags!

Ways of reducing the use of resources

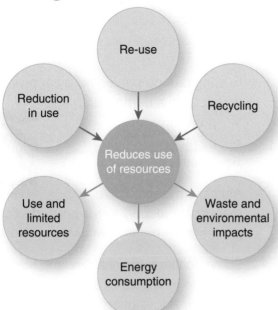

- Re-use
- Recycling
- Reduction in use
- **Reduces use of resources**
- Use and limited resources
- Waste and environmental impacts
- Energy consumption

Keywords

Life-cycle assessment ➤ An evaluation of the environmental impact of a product over the whole of its lifespan
Blast furnace ➤ Industrial method of extracting iron from iron ore

Quarrying

Many materials such as glass, metals, building materials, plastics and clay ceramics are produced from limited raw materials. Most of the energy used in their production comes from limited resources, such as fossil fuels. Obtaining raw materials from the earth by quarrying and mining has a detrimental environmental impact.

Some products, like glass, can be **reused** (e.g. washing and then using again for the same purpose). Recycled glass is crushed, melted and remade into glass products.

Blast furnace

Other products cannot be reused and so they are **recycled** for a different use.

Metals are recycled by sorting them, followed by melting them and recasting / reforming them into different products. The amount of separation required for recycling depends on the material (e.g. whether they are magnetic or not) and the properties required of the final product. For example, some scrap steel can be added to iron from a **blast furnace** to reduce the amount of iron that needs to be extracted from iron ore.

Recycling

Try to identify the environmental impact of this book by considering the effects of all of the stages of its life cycle.

1. What does a life-cycle assessment measure?
2. State two factors that a life-cycle assessment tries to evaluate.
3. Why are life-cycle assessments not always totally objective?
4. State one way in which we can reduce the use of resources.

Using materials

Corrosion and its prevention

Corrosion is the destruction of materials (e.g. metals) by chemical reactions by chemicals in the environment. Rusting is a common form of corrosion. It involves iron reacting with oxygen and water.

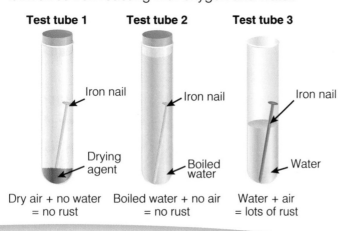

Test tube 1 — Iron nail, Drying agent
Dry air + no water = no rust

Test tube 2 — Iron nail, Boiled water
Boiled water + no air = no rust

Test tube 3 — Iron nail, Water
Water + air = lots of rust

Rusting can be prevented by applying a coating that acts as a barrier, such as…
- greasing
- painting
- electroplating.

Aluminium is a reactive metal that naturally forms an oxide coating which prevents the metal from further corrosion.

Some coatings are reactive and may contain corrosion inhibitors or a more reactive metal. For example, zinc is often used to **galvanise** iron. If the coating is then scratched, the zinc reacts instead of the iron. This is called **sacrificial protection**.

Magnesium blocks can be attached to a ship's hull to provide sacrificial protection.

Alloys as useful materials

Many of the metals we use every day are **alloys**. Pure metals such as gold, copper, iron and aluminium are too soft for many uses. Alloys are made by mixing metals together. This makes them harder and more suitable for everyday use.

100% pure **gold** (known as 24-carat gold) is often mixed with other metals. The proportion of gold in the alloy gives the carat rating (e.g. 18 carat contains 75% gold).	
Bronze (an alloy of copper and tin) is used to make statues and other decorative objects.	
Brass is an alloy of copper and zinc that is used to make water taps and door fittings.	
Steel is an alloy of iron, carbon and other metals such as chromium or nickel.	
High-carbon steel is strong but brittle – it is used to make cutting tools.	
Low-carbon steel is softer, so it can be more easily shaped. It is used to make car body panels.	
Steels containing nickel and chromium are known as **stainless steels** because of their resistance to corrosion. They are hard and are used to make cutlery and railway tracks.	
Aluminium alloys are strong and low in density. They are used in aerospace manufacturing, for example to make the bodies of aeroplanes.	

Ceramics

Everyday glass is soda-lime glass.

> sand + sodium carbonate + limestone → soda-lime glass

Borosilicate glass, made from sand and boron trioxide, melts at a higher temperature than soda-lime glass.

Clay ceramics, including pottery and bricks, are made by shaping wet clay and then heating it in a furnace.

Polymers

The properties of **polymers** depend on the monomer used to make the polymer and the conditions under which they are made. Low-density and high-density poly(ethene) are made from ethene, but using different catalysts and reaction conditions.

Thermosoftening polymers consist of individual polymer chains all tangled together which melt when heated. Thermosetting polymers consist of cross-links between the polymer chains and so they have a more rigid structure which means that they do not melt easily when they are heated.

Thermosoftening polymer (no cross-links)

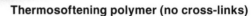

Thermosetting polymer

Cross-links

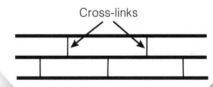

Find examples of ceramics, polymers and composite materials in your home.

Composites

Most **composite materials**, such as reinforced concrete, wood and fibreglass, consist of two materials: a matrix or binder and a reinforcement substance.

Some advanced composites are made from carbon fibres or carbon nanotubes instead of glass fibres.

Reinforced concrete column

Keywords

Galvanise ➤ Protect a metal by coating it with zinc

Alloy ➤ A mixture of metals

Polymer ➤ A large, long-chained molecule

Composite material ➤ Two (or more) different materials combined together

 **39**

1. State two ways of preventing corrosion.
2. What is an alloy?
3. What property does stainless steel have compared with ordinary steel?
4. Name the three raw materials used to make soda-lime glass.
5. What is the difference between the structures in thermosoftening and thermosetting polymers?
6. What is a composite material?

The Haber process and the use of NPK fertilisers

The Haber process

Ammonia (NH_3) is produced by the Haber process. The ammonia is used to make nitrogen-based **fertilisers**.

Ammonia is made by combining nitrogen (obtained by fractional distillation of liquid air) and hydrogen (from natural gas).

Fertiliser

nitrogen	+	hydrogen	$\rightleftharpoons$	ammonia
$N_{2(g)}$	+	$3H_{2(g)}$	$\rightleftharpoons$	$2NH_{3(g)}$

The purified gases are passed over an iron catalyst. The reaction is carried out at 450°C and 200 atmospheres pressure.

The reaction is reversible, so some of the ammonia produced will break down into nitrogen and hydrogen.

Upon cooling the ammonia liquefies and is removed. The unreacted nitrogen and hydrogen are recycled back into the reaction chamber.

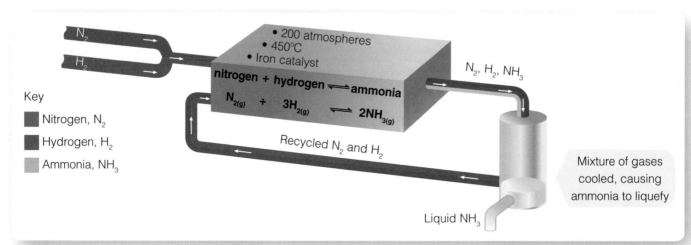

Key
- Nitrogen, N_2
- Hydrogen, H_2
- Ammonia, NH_3

- 200 atmospheres
- 450°C
- Iron catalyst

nitrogen + hydrogen $\rightleftharpoons$ ammonia

$N_{2(g)}$ + $3H_{2(g)}$ $\rightleftharpoons$ $2NH_{3(g)}$

N_2, H_2, NH_3

Recycled N_2 and H_2

Mixture of gases cooled, causing ammonia to liquefy

Liquid NH_3

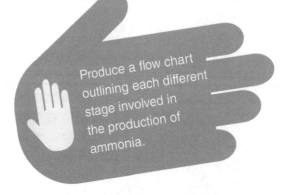

Produce a flow chart outlining each different stage involved in the production of ammonia.

Keyword

Fertiliser ➤ Any material added to the soil or applied to a plant to improve the supply of minerals and increase crop yield

Production and uses of NPK fertilisers

NPK fertilisers contain the elements nitrogen (chemical symbol **N**), phosphorus (**P**) and potassium (**K**). NPK fertilisers supply three important chemical elements that plants need and so the addition of NPK fertilisers improves agricultural productivity.

NPK fertilisers are formulations (see Module 29) of various salts containing appropriate percentages of N, P and K. Production of fertilisers can be achieved by using a variety of raw materials in several integrated processes.

Ammonia can be used to manufacture ammonium salts, such as ammonium sulfate $(NH_4)_2SO_4$ and nitric acid HNO_3.

Potassium chloride, potassium sulfate and phosphate rock are obtained by mining. Phosphate rock requires further processing as it is insoluble and so cannot be used directly as a fertiliser.

Phosphate rock is treated with nitric acid to make phosphoric acid (H_3PO_4) and calcium nitrate, $Ca(NO_3)_2$. Phosphoric acid is neutralised with ammonia to make ammonium phosphate.

$$H_3PO_4 + 3NH_3 \rightarrow (NH_4)_3PO_4$$

When phosphate rock is reacted with sulfuric acid, 'single super phosphate' is produced. This is a mixture of calcium phosphate and calcium sulfate.

If phosphate rock is reacted with phosphoric acid then 'triple superphosphate' calcium phosphate is produced.

HT Explaining the conditions used in the Haber process

The reaction to produce ammonia is exothermic:

$$N_{2(g)} + 3H_{2(g)} \rightleftharpoons 2NH_{3(g)} \qquad \Delta H = -92 \text{ kJmol}^{-1}$$

High temperatures favour endothermic reactions (see Module 24) so if the temperature is too high then the yield (amount produced) of ammonia will be low. If the temperature is too low then the yield of ammonia will be higher but the rate will be too slow. 450°C is a compromise temperature between rate and yield.

High pressure favours the reaction that produces fewer molecules of gas (in this case, high pressure favours the forward reaction, i.e. the production of ammonia). If the pressure is increased, the yield of ammonia and the rate of production will both increase but so will the cost of production. The increased revenue from the sale of the extra ammonia does not compensate for the additional costs. 200 atmospheres pressure is a compromise between yield, rate and cost.

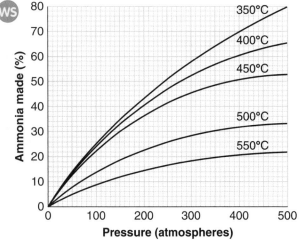

Different Haber process plants operate at slightly different conditions based upon…
➤ the availability and cost of raw materials and energy
➤ the demand for ammonia.

1. What are the raw materials needed to make ammonia?
2. Name the three chemical elements present in NPK fertiliers.
3. Name the compound formed when ammonia is reacted with phosphoric acid.

Mind map

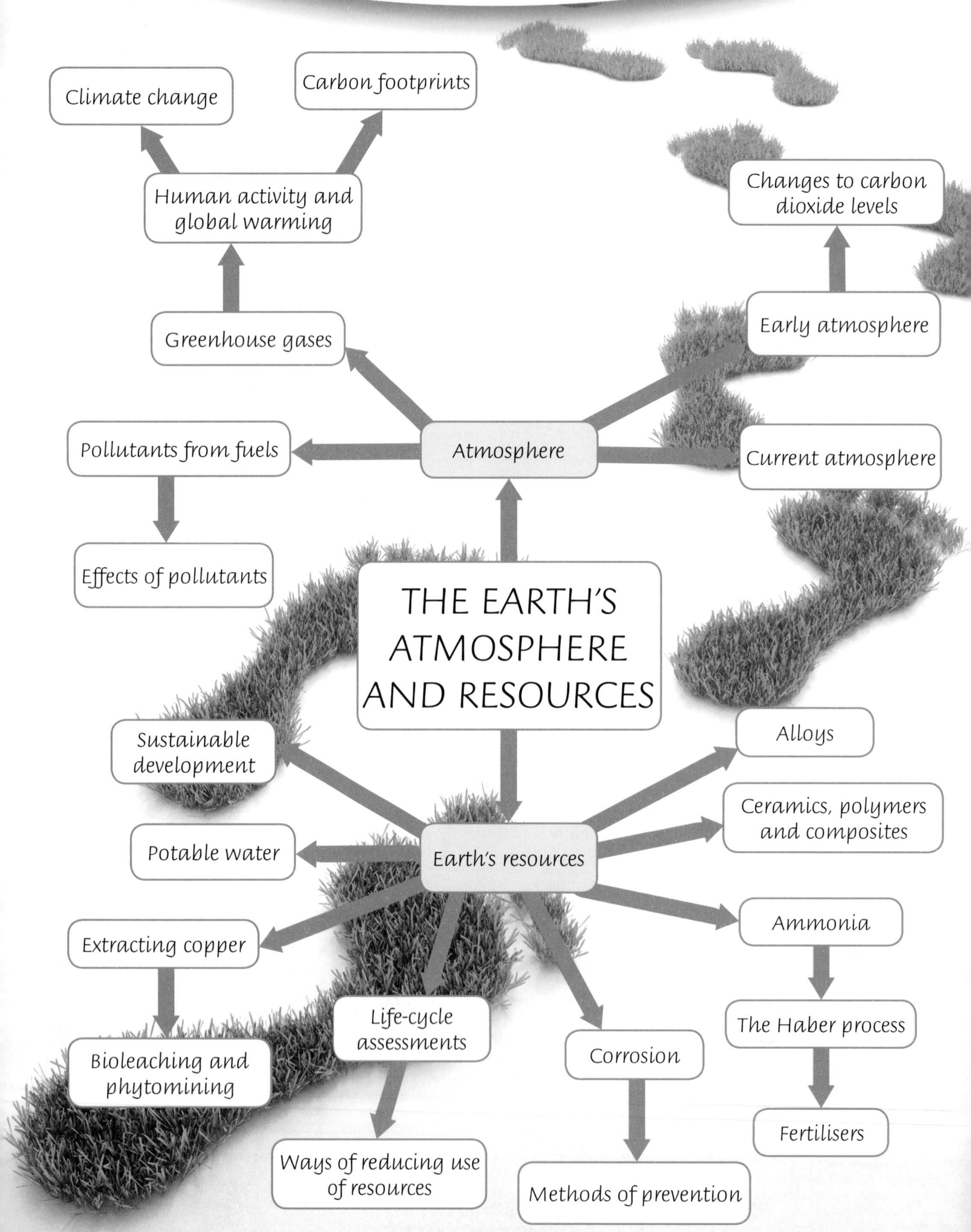

Climate change

Carbon footprints

Human activity and global warming

Changes to carbon dioxide levels

Greenhouse gases

Early atmosphere

Pollutants from fuels

Atmosphere

Current atmosphere

Effects of pollutants

THE EARTH'S ATMOSPHERE AND RESOURCES

Sustainable development

Alloys

Ceramics, polymers and composites

Potable water

Earth's resources

Extracting copper

Ammonia

Life-cycle assessments

Corrosion

The Haber process

Bioleaching and phytomining

Fertilisers

Ways of reducing use of resources

Methods of prevention

Practice questions

1. The composition of the Earth's atmosphere today is very different from how it was 4.6 million years ago. The pie charts below show the composition of the atmosphere today compared with millions of years ago.

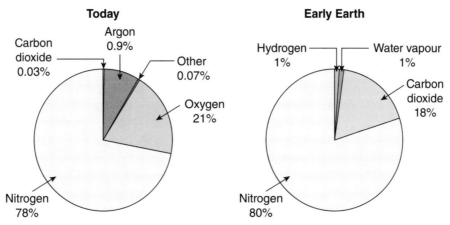

a) When the Earth was formed, where did many of the gases in the early atmosphere come from? **(1 mark)**

b) Name one gas whose composition has remained fairly constant over time. **(1 mark)**

c) Explain why oxygen is now present in the atmosphere and why it has not always been there. **(2 marks)**

d) Why is the amount of carbon dioxide in the atmosphere much lower today than in the early atmosphere? **(2 marks)**

e) Explain why the level of carbon dioxide in the atmosphere has been steadily increasing over the last couple of centuries. **(2 marks)**

2. Ammonia (NH_3) is an important gas used in the production of NPK fertilisers.
The equation for the production of ammonia is shown below.

$$N_{2(g)} + 3H_{2(g)} \rightleftharpoons 2NH_{3(g)}$$

a) Where are the raw materials for the production obtained from? **(2 marks)**

b) What conditions are typically used to manufacture ammonia? **(3 marks)**

c) Ammonia can be reacted with phosphoric acid (H_3PO_4) to make ammonium phosphate. Write a balanced symbol equation for this reaction. **(2 marks)**

Answers

Page 5
1. A compound.   2. Simple distillation.

Page 7
1. The plum pudding model suggests that the electrons are embedded within the positive charge in an atom. The nuclear model suggested that the positive charge was confined in a small volume (the nucleus) of an atom.
2. Because most of the positive charge passed straight through the atom. As only a few alpha particles were deflected, this suggested that the positive part of the atom was very small.
3. 6 protons, 6 electrons and 7 neutrons.
4. Isotopes.

Page 9
1. 2, 8, 1
2. He predicted that there were more elements to be discovered. He predicted their properties and left appropriate places in the periodic table based on his predictions.
3. A metal.

Page 11
1. Because they have full outer shells of electrons.
2. Lithium hydroxide and hydrogen.
3. The reactivity decreases.
4. Potassium bromide and iodine.

Page 13
1. **Any two from**: Transition metals have higher melting points (except for mercury); are more dense; are less reactive with water and oxygen.
2. **Any suitable example**: e.g. potassium manganite(VII): purple; copper(II) sulfate: blue.
3. Iron

Page 15
1. a) protons = 17 (**1 mark**), electrons = 17 (**1 mark**), neutrons = 18 (**1 mark**).
   b) 2, 8, 7 (**1 mark**).
   c) Similarity: same number of protons in each atom, same number of electrons in each atom, same chemical properties (**1 mark**). Difference: different number of neutrons in each atom (**1 mark**).
   d) **One from**: does not conduct heat/electricity; gas at room temperature (**1 mark**).
   e) $Cl_2 + 2NaI \rightarrow 2NaCl + I_2$ (**1 mark for correct formula, 1 mark for correct balancing**).
   f) Chlorine is less reactive than fluorine (**1 mark**), so it is unable to displace fluorine from a compound (**1 mark**).
2. a) Filtration (**1 mark**).
   b) Flask connected to condenser with bung/thermometer in place (**1 mark**).
      Water flowing in at the bottom and leaving at the top (**1 mark**).
      Salt water and pure water labelled (**1 mark**).

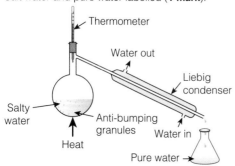

   c) The water is lost/evaporates during crystallisation (**1 mark**).

Page 17 (top right continuation)
3. $\frac{(10 \times 20) + (11 \times 80)}{100}$ (**1 mark**)
   = 10.8 (**1 mark**)
   Answer to 3 significant figures. (**1 mark**)

Page 17
1. Ionic.
2. Two.
3. A lattice (regular arrangement) of cations surrounded by a sea of (delocalised) electrons.

Page 19
1. Electrostatic forces/strong forces between cations and anions
2. Simple molecular, polymers, giant covalent
3.

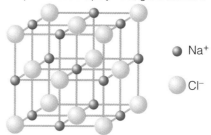

Page 21
1. The strength of the forces acting between the particles present.
2. The electrostatic forces of attraction between the ions are strong.
3. The intermolecular forces/forces between the molecules.
4. Polymers have larger molecules therefore there are more forces between the molecules.
5. There are lots of strong covalent bonds that need lots of energy to break them all.

Page 23
1. Because there are strong forces of attraction between the metal cations and delocalised electrons.
2. In alloys, the layers of metal ions are not able to slide over each other.
3. Each carbon atom has a spare electron that allows it to conduct electricity.
4. **Two from**: high tensile strength; high electrical conductivity; high thermal conductivity.
5. **Two from**: drug delivery into the body; lubricants; reinforcing materials.

Page 25
1. Less than 100 nm (1×10^{-7} m).
2. It increases by a factor of 10.
3. **Two from**: controlled drug delivery; synthetic skin; electronics; cosmetics and sun creams; development of new catalysts for fuel cell materials; in deodorants and fabrics to prevent the growth of bacteria.
4. **One advantage**: better skin coverage; more effective protection from the sun's UV rays. **One disadvantage**: potential cell damage in the body; harmful effects on the environment.

Page 27
1. a) Ionic (**1 mark**)
   b)

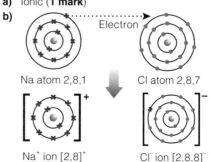

   (**Correct electronic structure of atoms, 1 mark; correct electronic structure of ions, 1 mark; correct charges on ions, 1 mark.**)

c) There are strong electrostatic forces of attraction (**1 mark**) between the ions (**1 mark**).

d) High (**1 mark**). Lots of energy is needed to overcome the forces holding the ions together (**1 mark**).

e)

  — Negatively charged chloride ions

+ Positively charged sodium ions (**1 mark**)

2. a) Covalent (**1 mark**).
   b) i) Two (**1 mark**).
      ii) Simple molecular (**1 mark**).
   c) i) Giant covalent (macromolecular) (**1 mark**).
      ii) Simple molecular structures consist of many individual molecules held together by weak intermolecular forces (**1 mark**). Giant covalent structures are lots of atoms all held together by covalent bonds (**1 mark**).
   d) Silicon dioxide will have a higher boiling point (**1 mark**). The covalent bonds in silicon dioxide that need to be broken in order to boil it are much stronger than the intermolecular forces that need to be broken in order to boil carbon dioxide (**1 mark**).

Page 29
1. The same.
2. a) 80   b) 58
3. Lower.

Page 31
1. 100 g
2. 124 g
3. Li_2O
4. P_4O_{10}

Page 33
1. 72%
2. **One from**: the reaction may not go to completion because it is reversible; some of the products may be lost when it is separated from the reaction mixture; some of the reactants may react in ways that are different to the expected reaction.
3. 45.9%.

Page 35
1. 2.3 g   2. 0.2 mol/dm³
3. 0.72 mol/dm³

Page 37
1. 0.0625   2. 9600 cm³ (9.6 dm³)
3. $Si + 2Cl_2 \rightarrow SiCl_4$

Page 39
1. a) Lower (**1 mark**), because the $CaCO_3$/calcium carbonate will have thermally decomposed meaning that some of the $CaCO_3$ will have decomposed into carbon dioxide, which will have gone into the air (**1 mark**).
   b) 100 (**1 mark**).
   c) 100 g of $CaCO_3$ forms 44 g of CO_2; therefore 10 g of $CaCO_3$ will have formed 4.4 g of CO_2 (**1 mark for working, 1 mark for the correct answer based on working; correct answer on its own scores 2 marks. The final answer must include the units**).
   d) moles of Mg: $0.15 \div 24 = 0.00625$ (**1 mark**); number of atoms: $0.00625 \times 6 \times 10^{23} = 3.75 \times 10^{21}$ (**1 mark**).
   e) $(0.2 \div 0.25) \times 100 = 80\%$ (**1 mark**).
2. a) $(22.50 \times 0.2) \div 1000 = 0.0045$ (**1 mark**).
   b) 0.0045 (**1 mark**); the ratio of moles of hydrochloric acid to sodium hydroxide in the equation is 1:1. This means that the number of moles of sodium hydroxide reacting is the same as the number of moles of hydrochloric acid (**1 mark**).
   c) $(0.0045 \times 1000) \div 25 = 0.18$ mol/dm³ (**1 mark for working, 1 mark for the correct answer based on the working; correct answer on its own scores 2 marks. The final answer must include the units**).

d) $0.18 \times 40 = 7.2$ g/dm³ (**1 mark for correct M_r of sodium hydroxide (40), 1 mark for the correct answer**).

Page 41
1. magnesium + oxygen → magnesium oxide
2. Sodium (because it is more reactive).
3. **Two from**: zinc, iron, copper.
4. Magnesium is being oxidised (because it loses electrons) and Zn^{2+} is being reduced (because it gains electrons).

Page 43
1. zinc + sulfuric acid → zinc sulfate + hydrogen.
2. Fe
3. A metal, metal oxide or metal carbonate.
4. Lithium nitrate.
5. Add solid until no more reacts, filter off the excess solid, crystallise the remaining solution.
6. Barium sulfate.

Page 45
1. An acid.
2. OH^-
3. $H^+_{(aq)} + OH^-_{(aq)} \rightarrow H_2O_{(l)}$
4. A strong acid fully ionises/dissociates in solution. A weak acid only partially ionises/dissociates in solution.
5. So that the ions are able to move.

Page 47
1. Potassium will be formed at the cathode; iodine will be formed at the anode.
2. Hydrogen will be formed at the cathode; iodine will be formed at the anode.
3. $4OH^- \rightarrow O_2 + 2H_2O + 4e^-$ (or $4OH^- - 4e^- \rightarrow O_2 + 2H_2O$).

Page 49
1. It cools down.
2.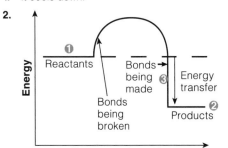

3. −1299 kJ (allow 1299 kJ).
4. Exothermic – more energy is released when bonds are made than is used up in breaking the bonds in the reactants/ΔH is negative.

Page 51
1. A system containing chemicals that react together to produce electricity.
2. A fuel cell has a constant supply of fuel; a chemical cell has the fuel contained within it and it is not replaced.
3. Water.
4. $4H^+_{(aq)} + O_{2(g)} + 4e^- \rightarrow 2H_2O_{(g)}$

Page 53
1. a) $2\,Zn_{(s)} + O_{2(g)} \rightarrow 2\,ZnO_{(s)}$ (state symbols are not required. **1 mark awarded for the correct symbols/formulae and for the equation being correctly balanced**).
   b) ZnO/zinc oxide (**1 mark**), because it loses oxygen (**1 mark**).
   c) Less reactive (**1 mark**); magnesium is able to displace zinc from zinc oxide, meaning that magnesium is more reactive than zinc (**1 mark**).
   d) By reduction with carbon (**1 mark**), because it is below carbon in the reactivity series (**1 mark**).
   e) Zinc (**1 mark**), because it loses electrons (**1 mark**).
2. a) A chemical cell where the source of fuel is supplied externally (**1 mark**).
   b) There is a constant supply of fuel in a fuel cell but not in a chemical cell (**1 mark**).

c)

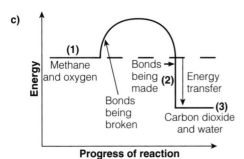

(**1 mark for each label numbered on the graph**.)

d) Bonds broken:

4 C–H: $4 \times 413 = 1652$ kJ

2 O=O: $2 \times 498 = 996$ kJ

Total = 2648 kJ (**1 mark**)

Bonds formed:

2 C=O: $2 \times 803 = 1606$ kJ

4 O–H: $4 \times 464 = 1856$ kJ

Total = 3462 kJ (**1 mark**)

ΔH = Bonds broken – bonds formed = 2648 – 3462

= – 814 kJ/mol (**1 mark for correct calculation, including correct sign**).

Page 55

1. 0.75 g/s

2. **Two from**: the concentrations of the reactants in solution; the pressure of reacting gases; the surface area of any solid reactants; temperature; presence of a catalyst.

3. By attaching a gas syringe and recording the volume of gas collected in a certain amount of time, e.g. volume collected every 10 seconds.

4. The rate increases.

Page 57

1. The idea that, for a chemical reaction to occur, the reacting particles must collide with sufficient energy.

2. The minimum amount of energy that the particles must have when they collide in order to react.

3. There are more particles in the same volume of liquid and so there are more chances of reactant particles colliding.

4. A species that speeds up a chemical reaction but is not used up during the reaction.

5. They provide an alternative pathway of lower activation energy.

Page 59

1. $\rightleftharpoons$

2. Endothermic.

3. **a)** The amount of nitrogen will decrease.

   b) The amount of nitrogen will decrease.

Page 61

1. **a)** 50 seconds (**1 mark**), as after this time no more gas was collected/the volume of gas did not change (**1 mark**).

   b) $40 \div 50 = 0.8$ cm³/s (working **1 mark**: allow $40 \div$ answer to part a; answer with units, **1 mark**).

   c) The gradient was steeper after 10 seconds than after 40 seconds. (**1 mark**)

   d)

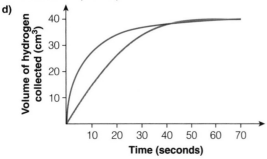

(**Curve is steeper than in original graph**, **1 mark**; **final volume is 40 cm³**, **1 mark**.)

e) At a higher concentration there will be more particles of acid in the same volume of solution (**1 mark**), and so there will be more/an increased probability/more likelihood of/collisions (**1 mark**).

2. **a)** The water in the equation appears as a gas (**1 mark**).

   b) That the reaction is reversible (**1 mark**).

   c) High pressure favours the reaction that produces the smaller number of molecules of gas; i.e. the reverse reaction will be favoured, which uses up hydrogen (**1 mark**).

   d) The yield of hydrogen will increase (**1 mark**); increasing temperature favours the endothermic (in this case forward) reaction (**1 mark**).

Page 63

1. Dead biomass.

2. Molecules that contain carbon and hydrogen atoms only.

3. Fractional distillation.

4. C_3H_8

5. $C_2H_6 + 3.5\,O_2 \rightarrow 2CO_2 + 3H_2O$ **or** $2C_2H_6 + 7\,O_2 \rightarrow 4CO_2 + 6H_2O$

Page 65

1. C_4H_{10}

2. C_nH_{2n}

3.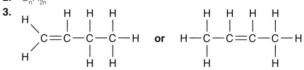

4. $C_2H_4 + Br_2 \rightarrow C_2H_4Br_2$

5. Ethanol.

Page 67

1. $CH_3CH_2CH_2OH$

2. $C_4H_9OH + 6O_2 \rightarrow 4CO_2 + 5H_2O$

3. As a fuel/solvent.

4.

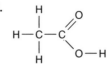

5. Ethyl ethanoate.

Page 69

1. They contain a carbon–carbon double bond.

2. Polypeptides/proteins.

3. It encodes genetic instructions for the development and functioning of living organisms and viruses.

Page 71

1. **a)** Dead biomass sinks to ocean bottom (**1 mark**); decaying biomass is covered in mud, which turns to rock (**1 mark**); biomass decays, slowly forming crude oil under the rock (**1 mark**).

   b) Fractional distillation (**1 mark**); the molecules in crude oil are separated according to their boiling points (**1 mark**).

   c) Saturated (**1 mark**); hydrocarbons/molecules with the general formula C_nH_{2n+2} (**1 mark**).

   d) Cracking turns relatively useless long-chain molecules (**1 mark**) into more useful products (**1 mark**).

   e) By passing the hydrocarbon vapour over a hot catalyst/mixing the hydrocarbon with steam at high temperatures (**1 mark**).

   f) C_4H_{10} (**1 mark**).

2. **a)** Addition polymerisation (**1 mark**).

   b) The carbon–carbon double bond (**1 mark**).

   c) **One from**: proteins; DNA; starch; cellulose (**1 mark**).

3. **a)** $C_2H_4 + H_2O \rightarrow C_2H_5OH$ (**1 mark for reactants; 1 mark for correct formula of ethanol – allow C_2H_6O**)

   b) Any acid, e.g. concentrated sulfuric acid (**1 mark**)

   c) Hydrogen (**1 mark**)

d) 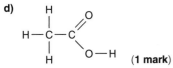(**1 mark**)

e) Ethyl ethanoate (**1 mark**)

Page 73
1. A single element or compound.
2. A mixture that has been designed as a useful product.
3. **Two from**: fuels; cleaning materials; paints; medicines; foods; fertilisers.
4. 0.55

Page 75
1. Oxygen.
2. Add a lit splint and there will be a squeaky pop.
3. Calcium hydroxide solution.
4. It turns milky.
5. It turns it red before bleaching it.

Page 77
1. Potassium.
2. Crimson red.
3. Magnesium hydroxide.
4. $Fe^{2+}(aq) + 2OH^-(aq) \rightarrow Fe(OH)_2(s)$
5. Green.

Page 79
1. The carbonate (CO_3^{2-}) ion.
2. Cream/off white.
3. Barium chloride solution.
4. **One from**: more accurate; more sensitive; can be used with very small sample sizes.

Page 81
1. **a)** K_2SO_4 (**1 mark**).
   b) Heat and then dip a piece of nichrome wire in concentrated hydrochloric acid to clean it (**1 mark**); dip the wire in the compound (**1 mark**); put the wire into a Bunsen burner and observe the colour of the flame (**1 mark**).
   c) Lilac (**1 mark**).
   d) Dilute hydrochloric acid (**1 mark**); barium chloride solution (**1 mark**).
   e) A white (**1 mark**) precipitate (**1 mark**).
   f) Flame emission spectrometer (**1 mark**).
2. **a)** Ca^{2+} (**1 mark**).
   b) Carbon dioxide (**1 mark**).
   c) CO_3^{2-} (**1 mark**).
   d) $CaCO_3$ (**1 mark**).
   e) Add dilute nitric acid (**1 mark**) followed by silver nitrate solution/ aqueous silver nitrate (**1 mark**) and a white precipitate/solid (**1 mark**) will be observed.

Page 83
1. **Two from**: carbon dioxide; water vapour; methane; ammonia; nitrogen.
2. As a product of photosynthesis.
3. Approximately $\frac{4}{5}$ or 80%.
4. Because it was used in photosynthesis and to form sedimentary rocks.

Page 85
1. **Two from**: water vapour; carbon dioxide; methane.
2. Increased animal farming/rubbish in landfill sites.
3. **Two from**: rising sea levels leading to flooding/coastal erosion; more frequent/severe storms; changes to the amount, timing and distribution of rainfall; temperature and water stress for humans and wildlife; changes in the food producing capacity of some regions; changes to the distribution of wildlife species.
4. **One from**: disagreement over the causes and consequences of climate change; lack of public information and education; lifestyle changes, e.g. greater use of cars and aeroplanes; economic considerations, i.e. the financial costs of reducing the carbon footprint; incomplete international cooperation.

Page 87
1. **Two from**: carbon dioxide; carbon monoxide; water vapour; sulfur dioxide; nitrogen oxides.
2. From the incomplete combustion of fossil fuels.
3. They cause respiratory problems and can form acid rain.

Page 89
1. Living such that the needs of the current generation are met without compromising the ability of future generations to meet their own needs.
2. Pure water has no chemicals added to it. Potable water may have other substances in it but it is safe to drink.
3. Filtered and then sterilised.
4. Distillation or reverse osmosis.

Page 91
1. **One from**: electrical wiring; water pipes.
2. We are running out of metal ores.
3. Bioleaching.
4. **One from**: displacement using scrap iron; electrolysis.

Page 93
1. The environmental impact of a product over the whole of its life.
2. **Two from**: how much energy is needed; how much water is used; what resources are required; how much waste is produced; how much pollution is produced.
3. Some of the values are difficult to quantify, meaning that value judgements have to be made which could be biased/based on opinion.
4. **One from**: using fewer items that come from the earth; reusing items; recycling more of what we use.

Page 95
1. **One from**: greasing; painting; electroplating; attaching a more reactive metal.
2. A mixture of metals.
3. It is more resistant to corrosion/rusting.
4. Sand, sodium carbonate and limestone.
5. Thermosetting polymers have cross-links between the polymer chains; thermoplastic polymers are just tangles of polymer chains.
6. Two (or more) different materials combined.

Page 97
1. Nitrogen and hydrogen.
2. Nitrogen, phosphorus, potassium.
3. Ammonium phosphate.

Page 99
1. **a)** Volcanoes (**1 mark**).
   b) Nitrogen (**1 mark**).
   c) Oxygen is formed by photosynthesis (**1 mark**); oxygen has not always been present in the atmosphere because green plants/ algae have not always existed (**1 mark**).
   d) Carbon dioxide is absorbed into the oceans/forms carbonate rocks (**1 mark**), and is used in photosynthesis (**1 mark**).
   e) There has been increased consumption of fossil fuels (**1 mark**), e.g. since the Industrial Revolution/greater use of transport such as cars which produce carbon dioxide when they burn fuel (**1 mark**).
2. **a)** Nitrogen is obtained from the fractional distillation of liquefied air (**1 mark**); hydrogen is obtained from natural gas (**1 mark**).
   b) 450°C (**1 mark**), 200 atmospheres (**1 mark**), an iron catalyst (**1 mark**).
   c) $3NH_3 + H_3PO_4 \rightarrow (NH_4)_3PO_4$ (**1 mark for correct formula of the three species in the equation**, **1 mark for a correctly balanced equation**).

The Periodic Table

Key

- Metals
- Non-metals

Element box layout:
- Relative atomic mass (top): 1
- Atomic symbol: H
- Name: hydrogen
- Atomic number (bottom): 1

1	2											3	4	5	6	7	0 or 8
																	4 **He** helium 2
7 **Li** lithium 3	9 **Be** beryllium 4											11 **B** boron 5	12 **C** carbon 6	14 **N** nitrogen 7	16 **O** oxygen 8	19 **F** fluorine 9	20 **Ne** neon 10
23 **Na** sodium 11	24 **Mg** magnesium 12											27 **Al** aluminium 13	28 **Si** silicon 14	31 **P** phosphorus 15	32 **S** sulfur 16	35.5 **Cl** chlorine 17	40 **Ar** argon 18
39 **K** potassium 19	40 **Ca** calcium 20	45 **Sc** scandium 21	48 **Ti** titanium 22	51 **V** vanadium 23	52 **Cr** chromium 24	55 **Mn** manganese 25	56 **Fe** iron 26	59 **Co** cobalt 27	59 **Ni** nickel 28	63.5 **Cu** copper 29	65 **Zn** zinc 30	70 **Ga** gallium 31	73 **Ge** germanium 32	75 **As** arsenic 33	79 **Se** selenium 34	80 **Br** bromine 35	84 **Kr** krypton 36
85 **Rb** rubidium 37	88 **Sr** strontium 38	89 **Y** yttrium 39	91 **Zr** zirconium 40	93 **Nb** niobium 41	96 **Mo** molybdenum 42	[98] **Tc** technetium 43	101 **Ru** ruthenium 44	103 **Rh** rhodium 45	106 **Pd** palladium 46	108 **Ag** silver 47	112 **Cd** cadmium 48	115 **In** indium 49	119 **Sn** tin 50	122 **Sb** antimony 51	128 **Te** tellurium 52	127 **I** iodine 53	131 **Xe** xenon 54
133 **Cs** caesium 55	137 **Ba** barium 56	139 **La*** lanthanum 57	178 **Hf** hafnium 72	181 **Ta** tantalum 73	184 **W** tungsten 74	186 **Re** rhenium 75	190 **Os** osmium 76	192 **Ir** iridium 77	195 **Pt** platinum 78	197 **Au** gold 79	201 **Hg** mercury 80	204 **Tl** thallium 81	207 **Pb** lead 82	209 **Bi** bismuth 83	[209] **Po** polonium 84	[210] **At** astatine 85	[222] **Rn** radon 86
[223] **Fr** francium 87	[226] **Ra** radium 88	[227] **Ac*** actinium 89	[261] **Rf** rutherfordium 104	[262] **Db** dubnium 105	[266] **Sg** seaborgium 106	[264] **Bh** bohrium 107	[277] **Hs** hassium 108	[268] **Mt** meitnerium 109	[271] **Ds** darmstadtium 110	[272] **Rg** roentgenium 111							

Elements with atomic numbers 112–116 have been reported but not fully authenticated

*The lanthanoids (atomic numbers 58–71) and the actinoids (atomic numbers 90–103) have been omitted.

The relative atomic masses of copper and chlorine have not been rounded to the nearest whole number.